Old Coldingham & St. Abb[...]
by Lawson Wood

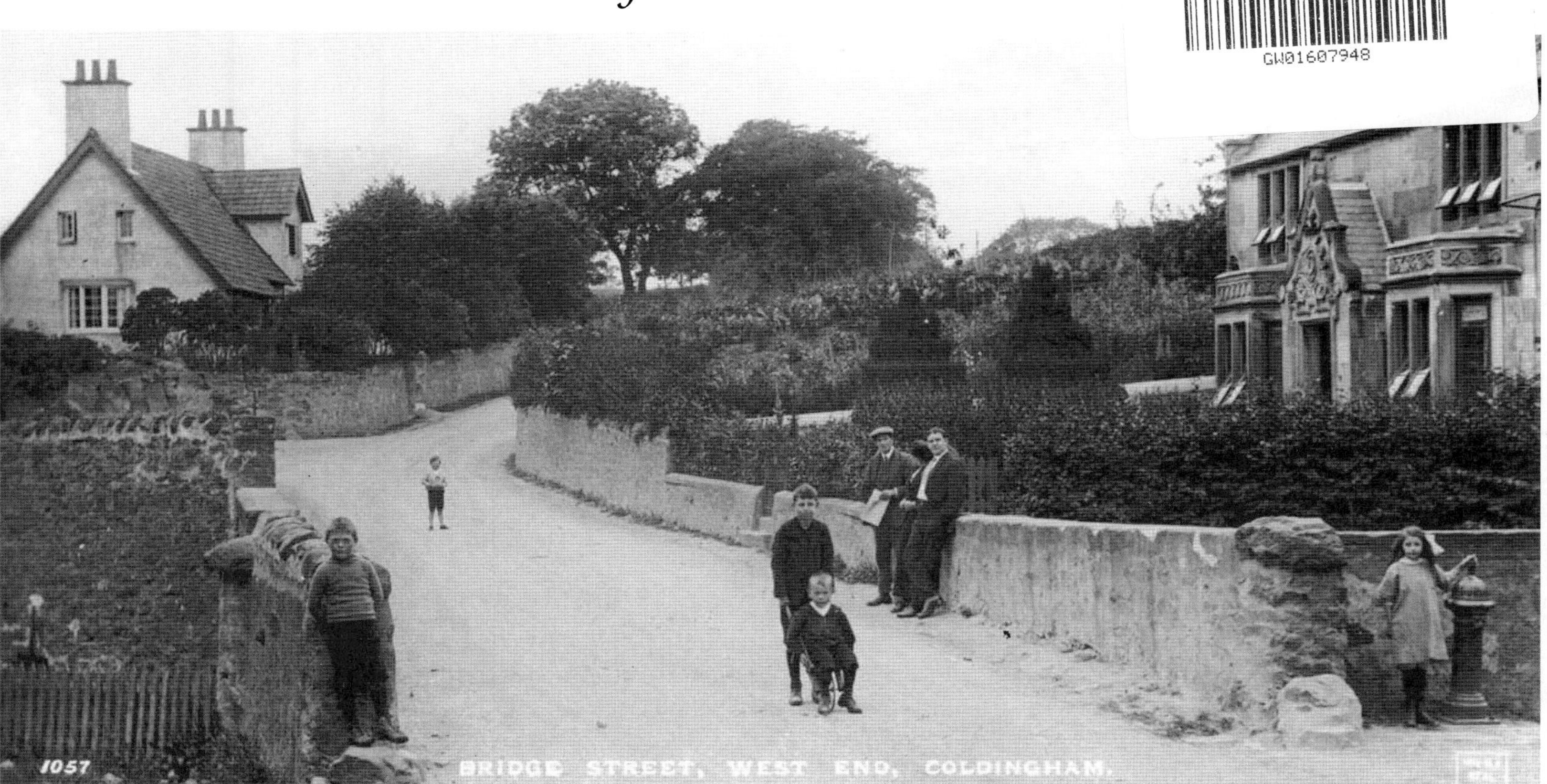

Bridge Street at the west end of Coldingham has changed little over the years due to the constriction of the road as it turns to the south towards Eyemouth and straight on west towards Reston and the A1 trunk road. There is a small bridge over the burn, and a point of interest is the drinking water point to the right of the photograph, this area of Coldingham still being known as 'Paradise'. A small narrow road veers off to the south, just before you pass over the bridge; this area comes around to the rear of Coldingham Abbey and is known as The Bow.

Text © Lawson Wood, 2009.
First published in the United Kingdom, 2009,
by Stenlake Publishing Ltd.
Telephone: 01290 551122
www.stenlake.co.uk
ISBN 9781840334456

ACKNOWLEDGEMENTS

Much of this book is dedicated to the lives of two local men, John Wood & Robbie Nisbet who took up the challenge of the new-fangled cameras and steadily went about recording local life in all its aspects. These were the first commercial photographers in the villages and coupled with Robert McIvor in Eyemouth, they were a formidable group. The postcards of Robbie Nisbet are readily available at old postcard fairs and most people have a large number in their collection, as he was such a prodigious producer of photographs to satisfy the demand of the many visiting tourists. On the other hand John Wood's collection lay dusty and deteriorating for over 70 years before it was rescued by Bob Thomson. I am indebted to Bob & Mary Thomson from Coldingham for their help and information so readily given; Alistair Crowe, operations manager of the St. Abbs Lifeboat gave me great insight into the role of the lifeboat; Gus Skene helped in identifying some of the old fishing boats, Gus has a superb collection of old postcards, photographs and other historic ephemera; The Shore Museum; Eyemouth Museum; Bill Cormack and the many local worthies who still have wonderful stories to tell of times gone by.

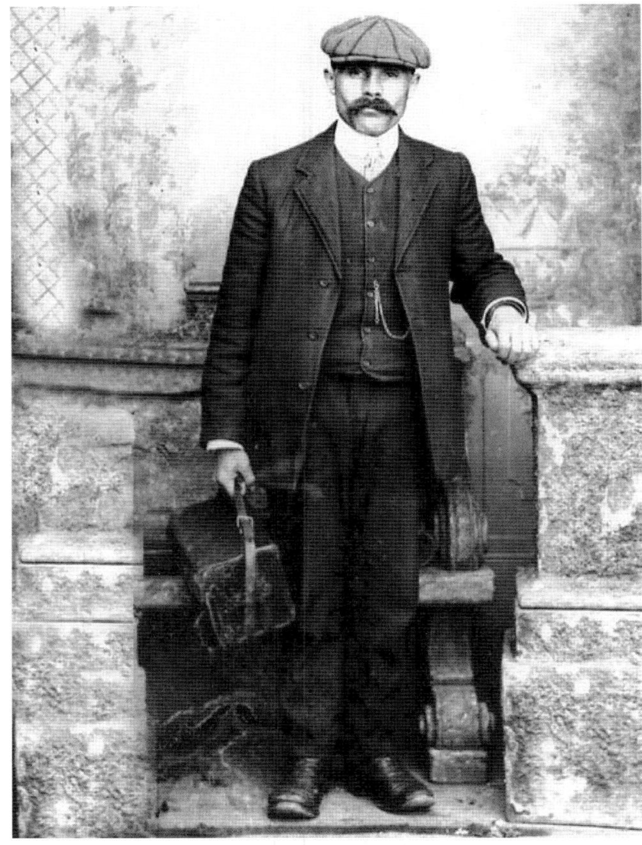

John Wood was probably the first commercial photographer to set up business in Coldingham. Not only did he possess a natural talent, he had a love for the farmland and coastline in this incredibly scenic area of south east Scotland. Born in 1854 at Old Scarlaw Farm in the Lammermuir Hills near Longformacus, he originally trained as a master joiner in Glasgow and moved to Coldingham some time during the 1880s where he married Margaret Kerr, who had the High Street shop at that time. He died in 1914 leaving a tremendous legacy of old half-plate glass negatives, several of which are reproduced in this volume with kind thanks to their curator Bob Thomson of Coldingham. The photographs were discovered in a garden shed which had lain undisturbed for over 75 years. Many were beyond repair and others were badly spoiled, but the information recorded in them by John Wood is an invaluable insight into the lives of these village folk at the turn of the last century. The other principal photographer who resided in St. Abbs was Robbie Nisbet, the sub-postmaster and general merchant in St. Abbs. His son, also Robbie Nisbet, continued to chronicle daily life and the father and son team produced many splendid postcards of Coldingham and St. Abbs.

INTRODUCTION

Coldingham and St. Abbs are both the product of Coldingham Priory. The priory also owned land both at Coldingham Shore and Eyemouth. Originally founded by King Edgar in 1098 A.D., the priory was originally known as the Church of St Mary Coldingham and was constituted as a cell of Durham Cathedral. At one time the priory provided the right to sanctuary for 37 days for any person who sought refuge within their lands. Extending over three miles inland, the perimeter of the priory's influence was marked by a 'Cross' at each of the road junctions, the names of Applin Cross, Friar's Cross, Crosslaw, Whitecross and Cairncross still appearing on local maps. Religion was not new to the area, as the Venerable Bede first described a monastic settlement on Coldburgh (now St. Abbs) Head back in 679 A.D. Although it was described as a Monastery of Virgins, there were reputed to be monks there too. However, the sister in charge, Æbbe (or Ebba) was the daughter of Æthelfrith and sister to the celebrated Oswald and Oswiu, both kings of Northumberland. Around 683 A.D., the settlement was supposedly attacked by marauding and 'licentious' Scots/Danes/English/German mercenaries (it is unclear who the perpetrators were, other than that their actions were recorded) attacked the monastery and the virgin nuns within their walls literally "cut of their noses to spite their faces" to render themselves unattractive to their assailants. However, evidence suggests that Æbbe was already dead at that time and that much of her history is entwined with that of her brothers and father. Whatever the cause, the monastery burned down at that time and was never rebuilt.

Coldingham first appeared on Ptolemy's Roman map of Britain and was named Colonia. Coldingham Shore, now St. Abbs, was the closest area with deep sheltered water with protective rocks from where the small fishing craft of Coldingham's inhabitants could be stored safely. The locals walked down the Fisher's Brae from the centre of Coldingham, where they connected to the Creel Path which led to Coldingham Shore, St. Abbs is still known locally as 'The Shore'. Boats were also stored in a couple of small bays to the north of the present day harbour and known as Horse Castle Bay and Burnmouth Harbour. (Burnmouth, as we know is a small fishing village to the south of Eyemouth, over seven miles away by road).

St. Abbs village originally consisted of 'Rock House' (the original clat and clay building from around the early 1700s was destroyed during a particularly severe storm in the late 1880s, before the protective harbour was built) and a small group of houses, known as the Under Row. Their inhabitants paid feus to Henry Home Drummond Esq. through his tenant, the Lord of the Manor, Mr. Brodie, who resided in Northfield House. Mr. Drummond always had a keen interest in the welfare of the locals and helped in any way he could. After Mr. Usher (of Usher Vaux Brewers and Distillers fame) bought the estate, he changed the village forever.

Like so many of the coastal fishing villages in the late 1800s, St. Abbs was also devastated on Black Friday, 14 October 1881, when 189 East Coast fishermen lost their lives in what can only be described as a storm of Biblical proportions. That day, St. Abbs and Coldingham lost three men and Eyemouth, 129. Burnmouth lost twenty-four, the Cove at Cockburnspath lost eleven, Newhaven fifteen and Fisherrow, seven.

Mr Usher was responsible for the construction of the outer harbour, which was opened in 1890 as a direct result of the storm of 1881. It formed a protective breakwater for the fishing boats, allowing them to remain in the water at all times, instead of having to be hauled out daily. The original or inner harbour was built in 1833 and was said to have had sixteen fishing craft. Their catches were taken by horse & cart to the markets in Edinburgh. Further improvements were made in 1849/1850. Andrew Usher was also responsible for the school, the church and the church hall. Many fine houses were added to the expanding village and soon the original 'Upper Row', first built in 1837 by Mr. Herriot, the farmer at Northfield, were superseded by more homes behind as well as the townhouses along Briery Law.

The original fish curing buildings were built around 1855 and had to be 'built like a fort' as all of their exterior gable walls were within the high water mark and were constructed on ancient bedrock. Although permission to build homes and business premises were granted by the landowners, once the property was completed the owners still had to pay a feu duty to them.

The tragic loss of lives from the Danish coastal drifter *Alfred Erlandsen*, and the distances that had to be traveled to the St. Abbs area from either Eyemouth or Dunbar, resulted in St. Abbs receiving its own lifeboat. The first lifeboat, the *Helen Smitten* was launched in 1911 and this selfless service still continues today the Crowes having provided over 200 years of service between the family members.

Coldingham remained as a compact cluster of homes and businesses spreading out and around the land controlled by Coldingham Priory, held in check by the nature of the land itself. The Town Cross is the junction of three roads, south and west to Eyemouth and Reston, north to Coldingham Moor, Cockburnspath and onwards to Edinburgh and east to St. Abbs and St. Abbs Head. Some 21 local traders had businesses in the village at the turn of the last century and it had two pubs, several boarding houses and even a brewery. Now with two holiday caravan parks and new housing estates, it is still a 'busy wee toon'.

Both Coldingham and St. Abbs are inexorably linked by their history, their culture and by their village folk. Still small and unassuming the villages have had to come to terms with the fact they are of incredible historic importance, as well as being picture postcard perfect. St. Abbs is home to one of the finest National Nature Reserves on mainland Britain and this stretch of the Berwickshire coastline also hosts the St. Abbs and Eyemouth Voluntary Marine Nature Reserve, the first marine preserve of its kind in Scotland.

I have tried not to reproduce photographs in this volume which have appeared in other publications, but in some cases, the imagery is so strong and so evocative of life over 100 years ago, that I felt that they just had to be included.

Lawson Wood, St. Abbs, 2009

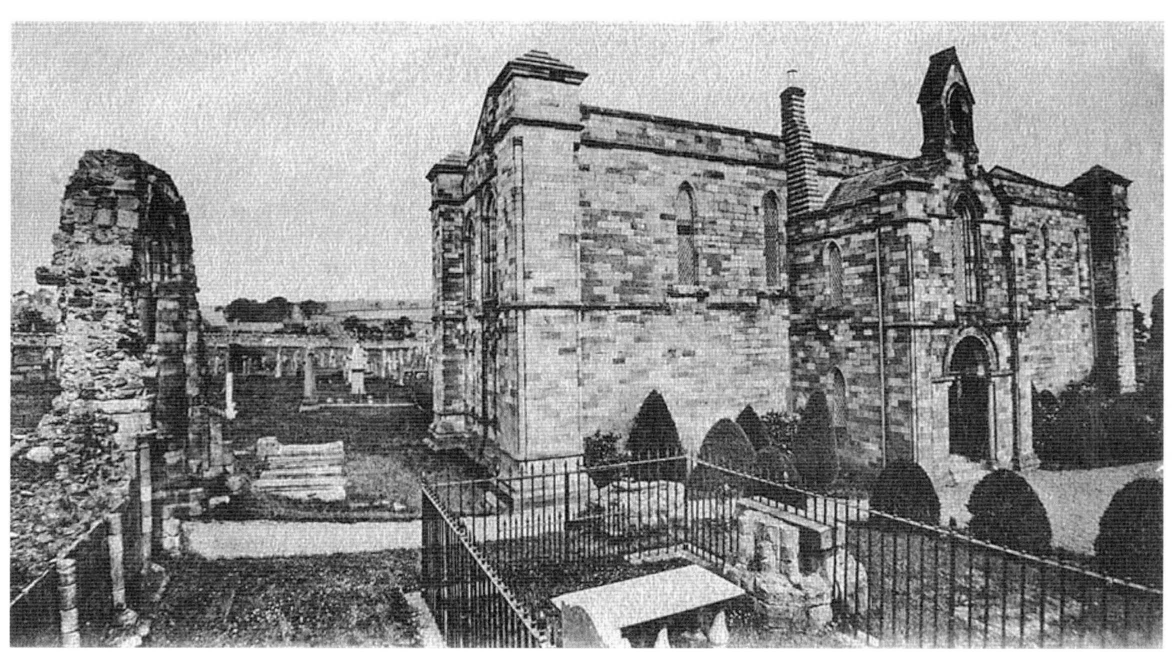

One of the more notable priors of Coldingham was John Stuart, brother of Mary, Queen of Scots, who was a regular visitor. Mary spent her last few days of freedom near to Coldingham in the sea fortress of Fast Castle, just north of St. Abbs Head. The priory was disjoined from Durham Cathedral in 1509 and was decreed by the Pope to be placed under the jurisdiction of Dunfermline Abbey. Burned down and ravaged on many occasions during the long and bloody wars between Scotland and England, it was only saved from total destruction when Oliver Cromwell (a Mason of very high order) discovered that Coldingham Priory had many Masonic tombs and inscriptions. The north wall and gable end were left standing. Coldingham Priory was rebuilt in 1831 and has served many different denominations over its colourful, yet chequered history.

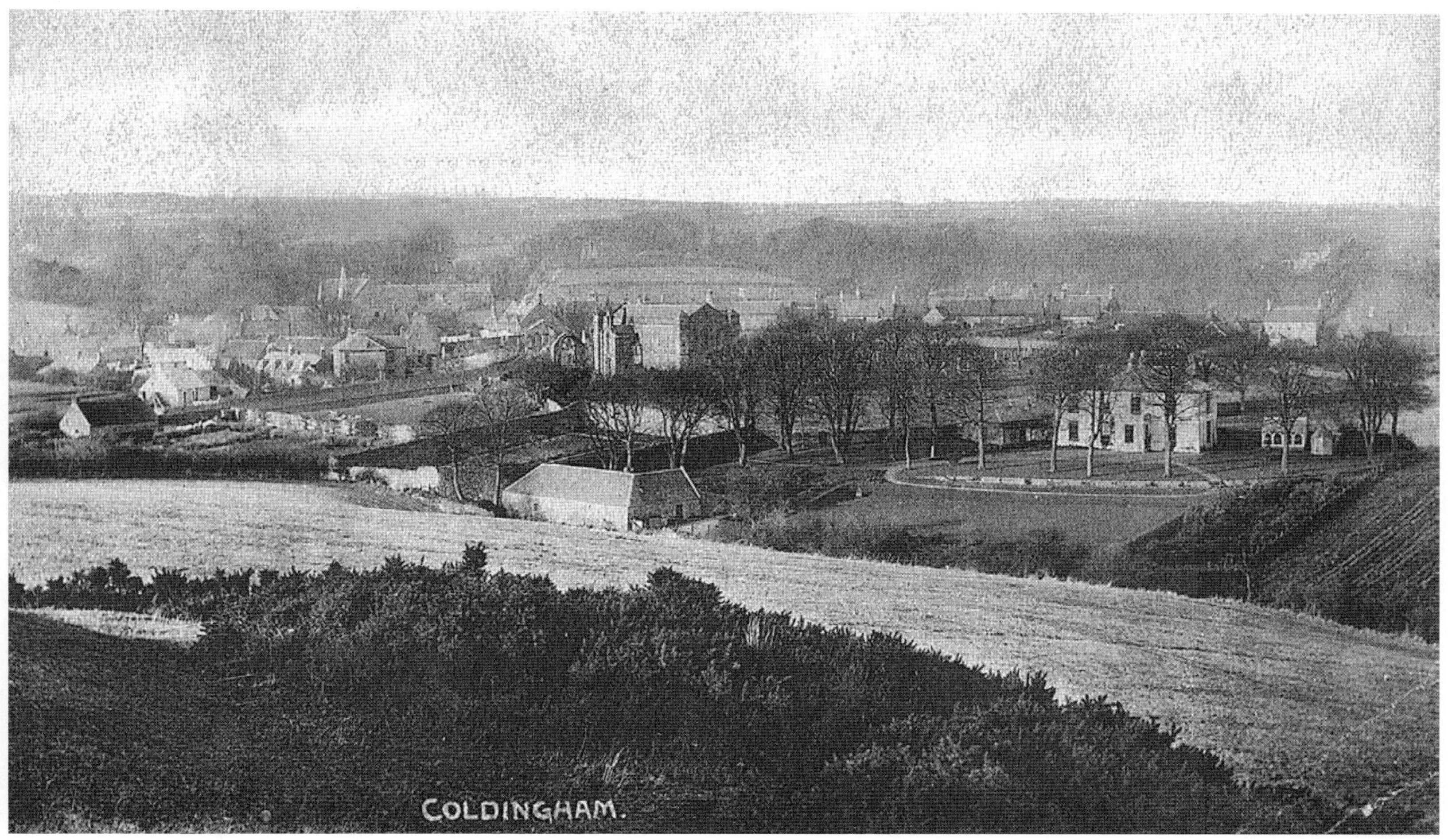

Viewed from Coldingham Law, a sleepy Coldingham during the winter months with the trees bare and offering clear sight of Coldingham Priory and the surrounding land. The view from the Law was particularly popular with photographers and with the village nestled in a cold vale. The Saxon name Colaunham is possibly one of the derivations for the roots of Coldingham. Historically we know that there was a village during the Roman occupation, hardly surprising really with two sources of fresh water, a sheltered small valley and access to a wide and safe, sandy beach, perfect for the flat-bottomed Roman galleys.

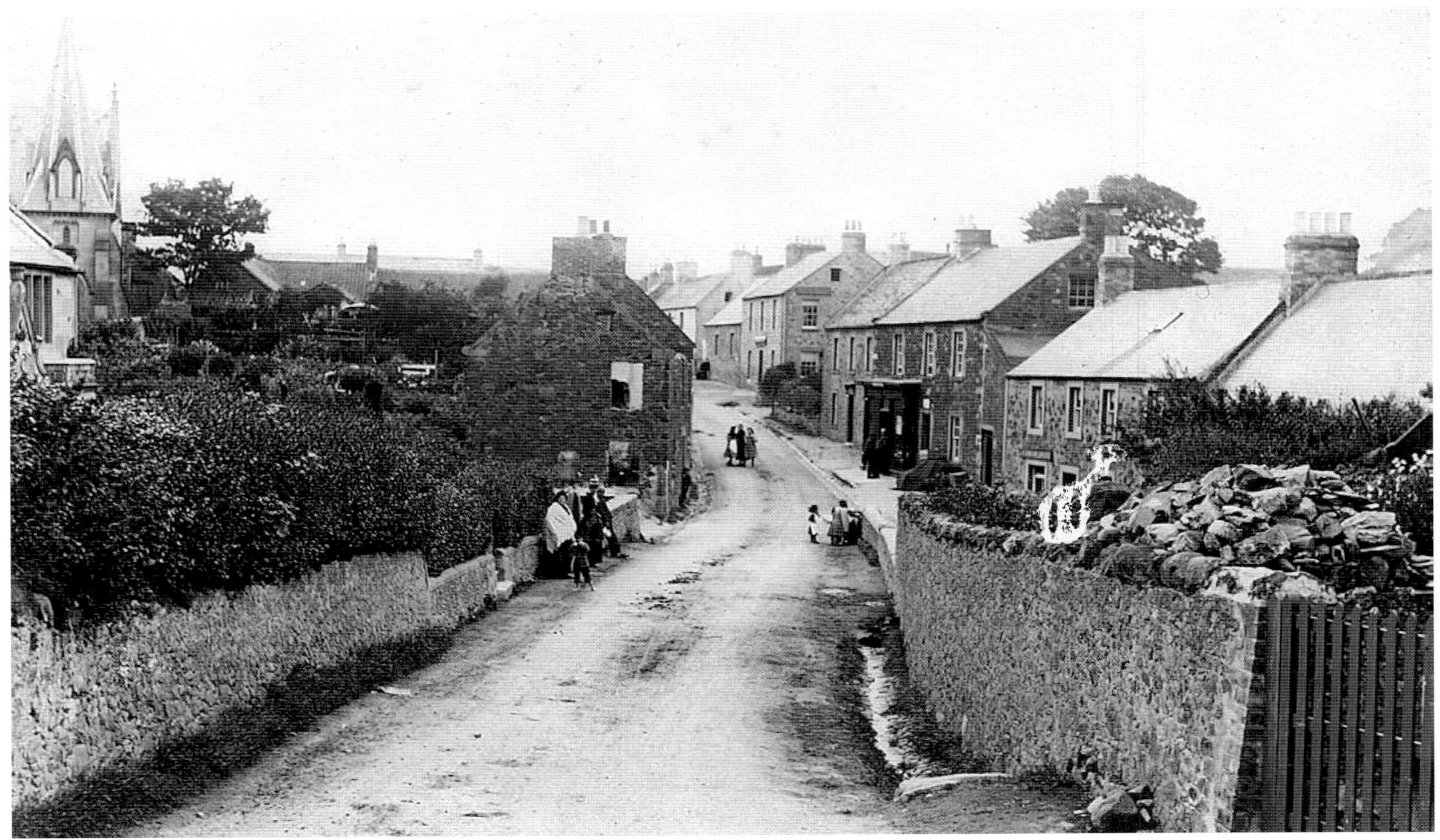

Looking east along Bridge Street, from the tight corner for travelling west to Reston or south to Eyemouth, little change has taken place apart from the old church which was torn down many years ago, after having been abandoned to the elements. In all of our local towns and villages the churches are subject to dwindling congregations and the rising costs of expenditure on repairs and upkeep. The wall to the right of the photograph (before you pass over the Burn Bridge) has now been removed, partly to allow for better line of sight for vehicles as they drive around the corner and also to facilitate a new entrance to a house which has recently been extended.

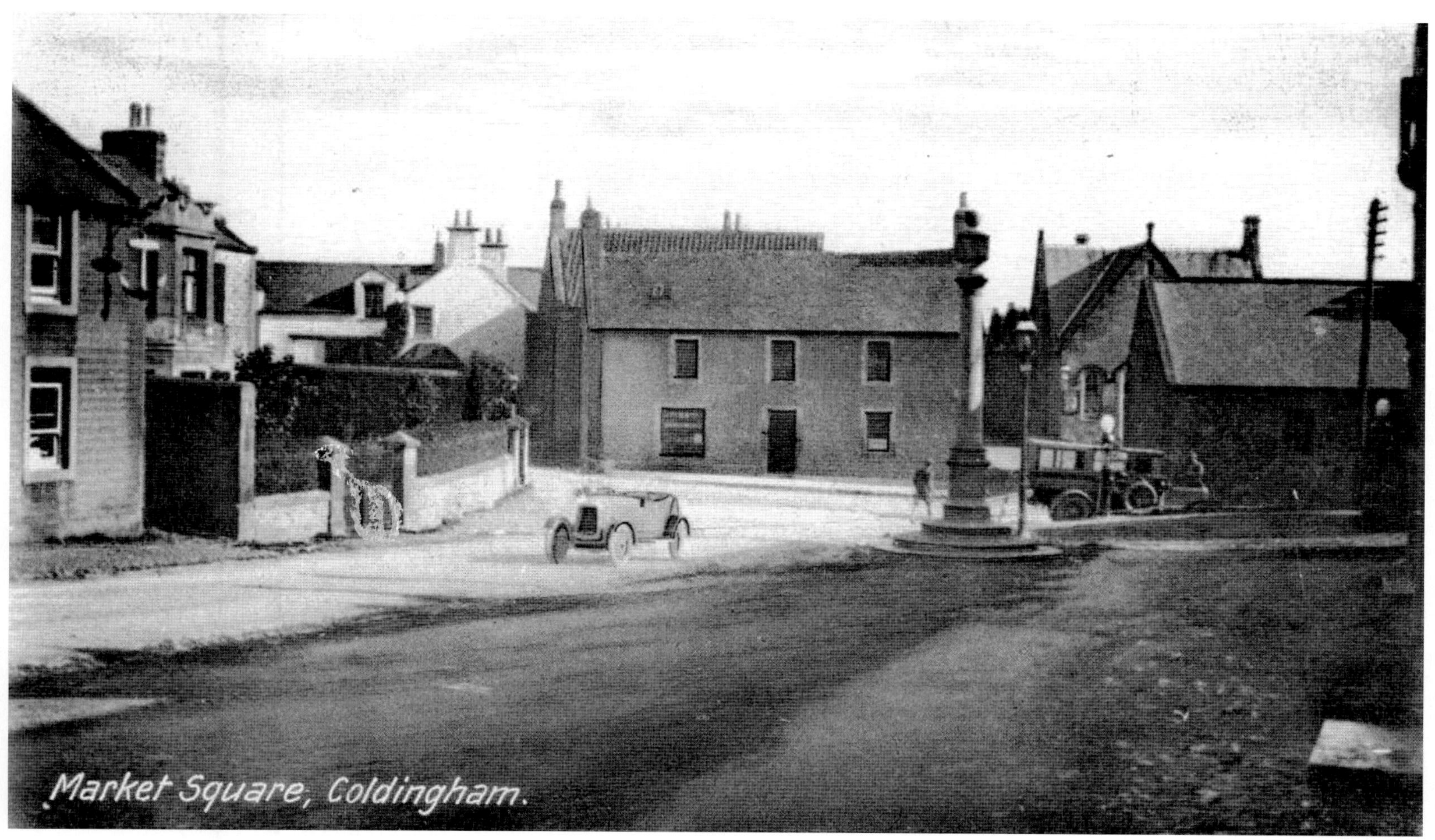

One of the older photographs of Coldingham village square or cross. Looking down Coldingham Main Street, past the Anchor Inn on the left and the New Inn to the far right (originally known as the New Hotel), in the centre of the photograph is the building once known as the 'Blue House'. It was so named because of the particular type of slate used on the roof, as the norm until then had been the orange pan-tile type of roof covering or even thatch. There was a small brewery in behind this building. The St. Abbs Road, whilst still very restricted at the corner, was even more so when these buildings were still in place. There is now a car park and entry to Coldingham Priory where these buildings once stood.

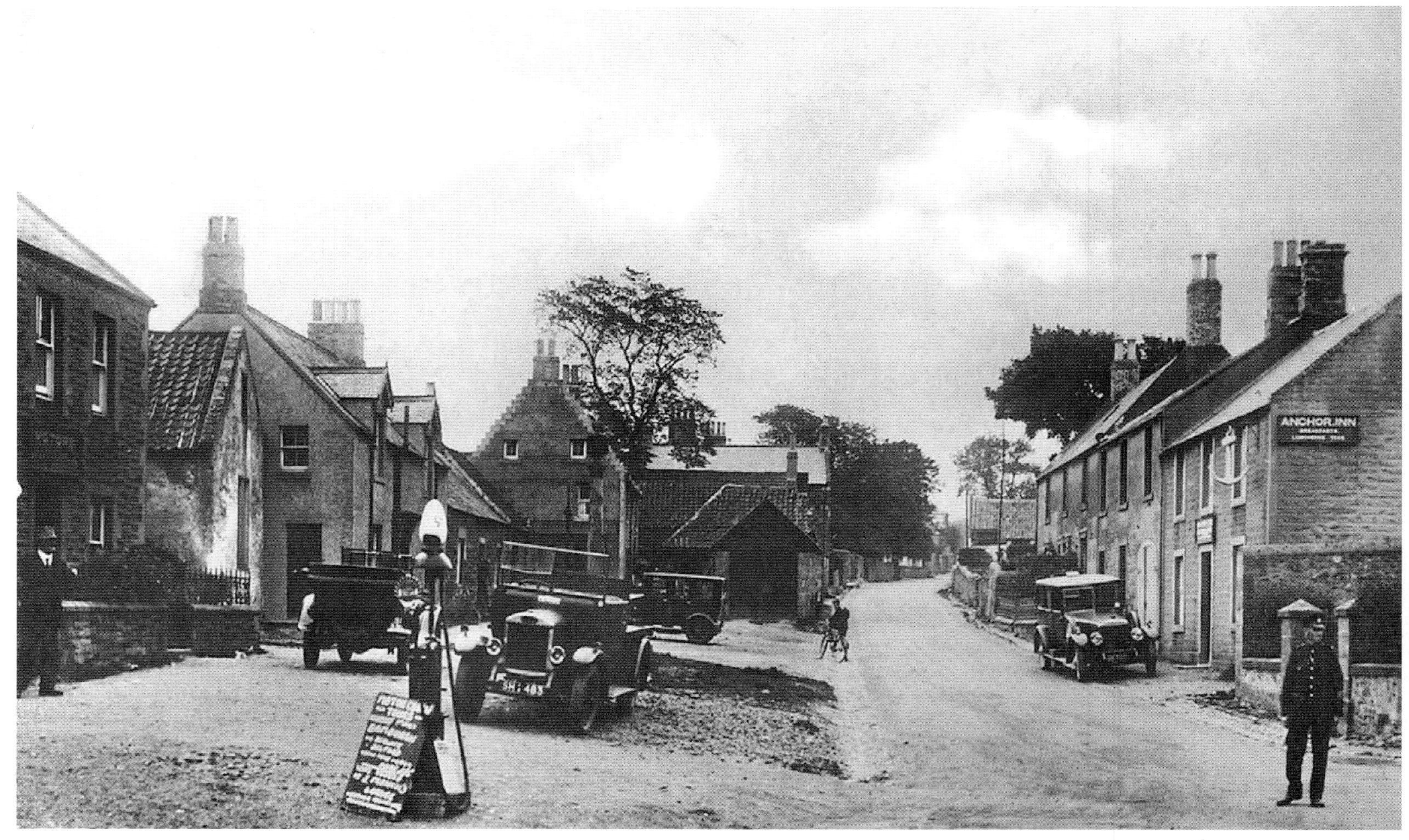

Coldingham Cross or Crossgate and looking up Main Street (now known as School Road). The Anchor Inn, located to the right of the photograph, is the oldest established public bar and restaurant and still continues to look after its clientele. To the left is the building belonging to James French – Coach Hirer. James French originally carried passengers by horse and cart, before motorized transport became more popular and he ran a regular service to meet the train at Reston Station. French's Garage is still on the same site and they still hire coaches to this day.

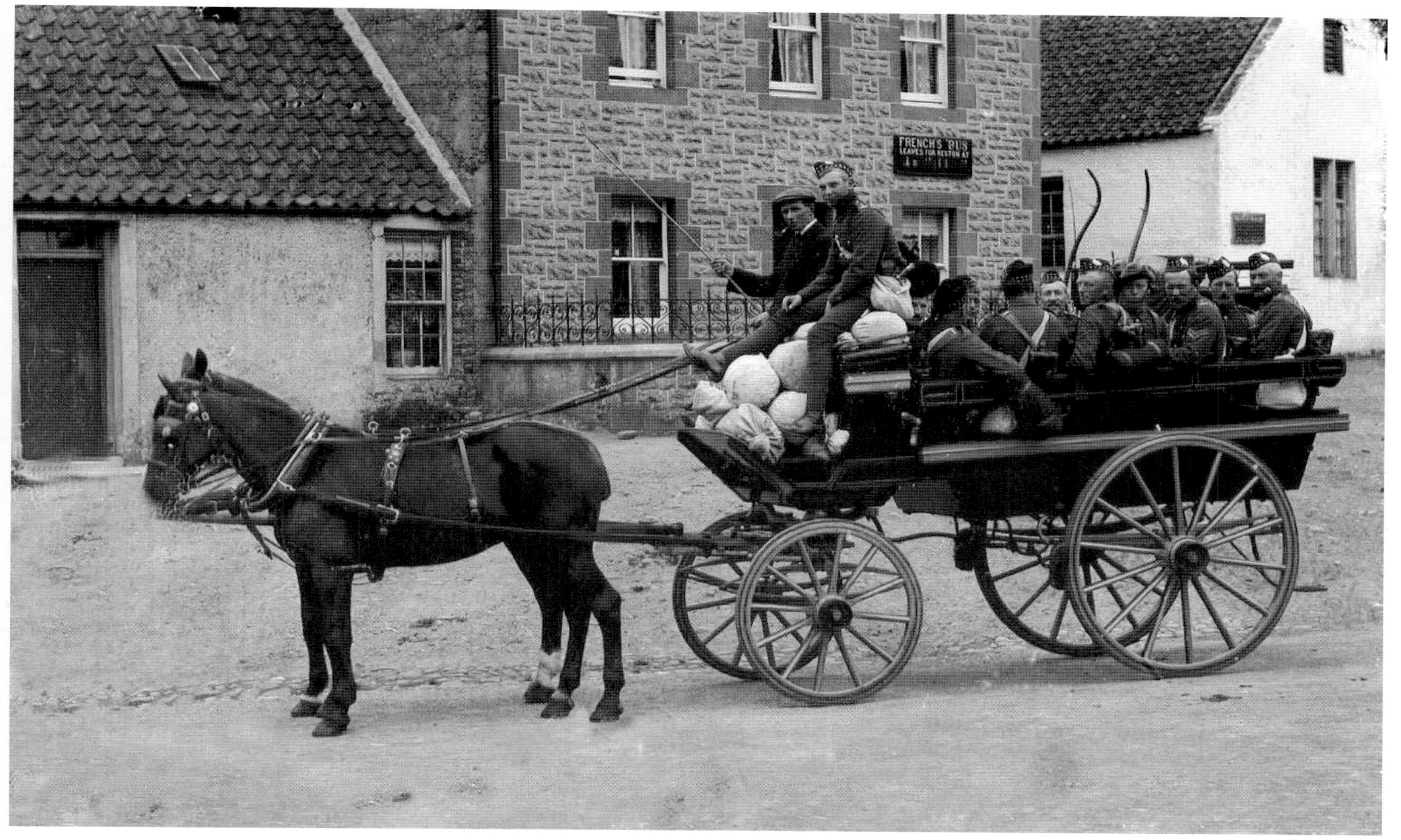

The Coldingham Volunteers about to set off to summer camp. The Territorial Army were a particularly strong force in the coastal towns and came under the jurisdiction of the Coldstream Guards which were based primarily at the Berwick upon Tweed barracks. These volunteers would be travelling by horse drawn cart to Reston Station where they would board a train to Berwick. It is unlikely that they would travel the entire ten miles to the barracks by horse and cart. This early 'bus' was supplied by James French. The sign on the back wall states "French's Bus, leaves for Reston at......"

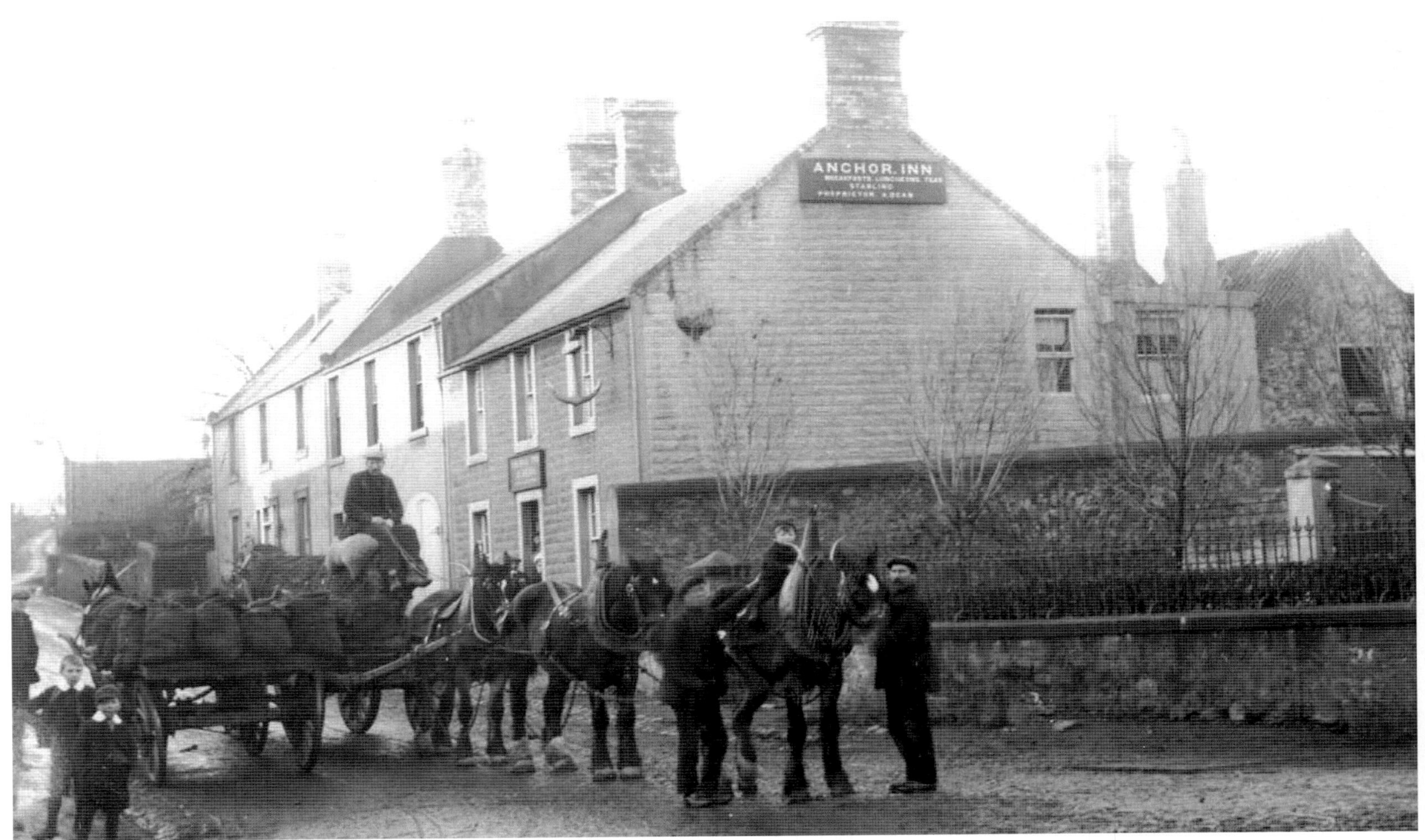

Another very fine record of village life, photographed by John Wood. Photographers always attracted attention and when two carts with horses were causing a 'traffic jam' in the high street, then this has had to be recorded. The local coal lorry, pulled by a single nag is aiming up what is now School Road, the other cart has part of a massive tree trunk and is being pulled by three very fine Clydesdale horses. Curiously there is a child on the back of the lead horse, more likely placed just for the photograph, as all the other children in view are smartly dressed in their 'Sunday Best' with starched white collars over dark jackets and wearing shoes. The road looks slick with mud and the Anchor Inn stands proud to the side.

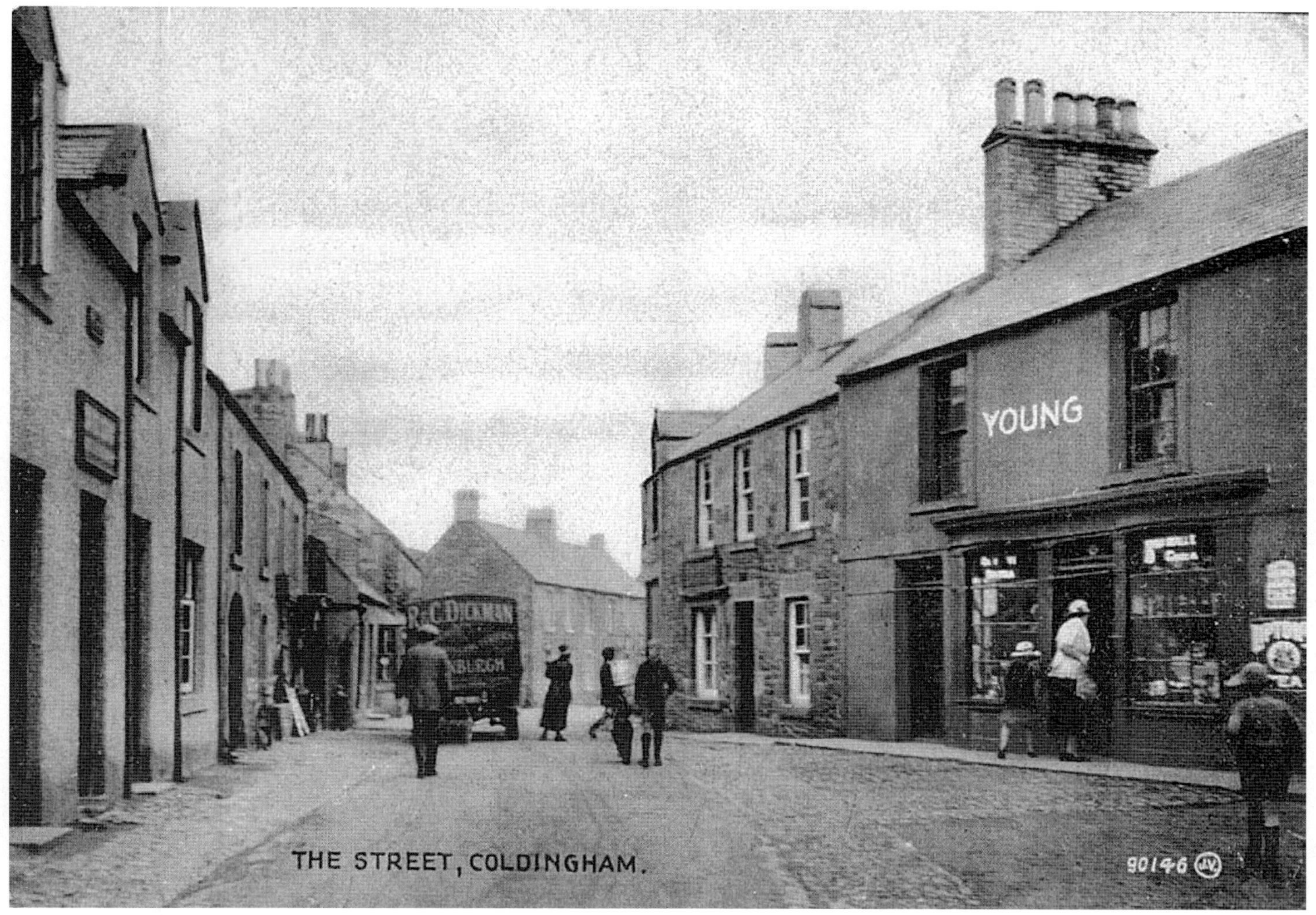

Around the time that this photograph was taken there were 21 licensed traders in Coldingham. "The Street", now known as St. Abbs Road, had quite a number of traders. This view is looking down towards the coast and has a visiting trader's van parked on the roadside; R & C Dickman of Edinburgh were a company of general suppliers to the local shop owners who visited the town and surrounding area weekly.

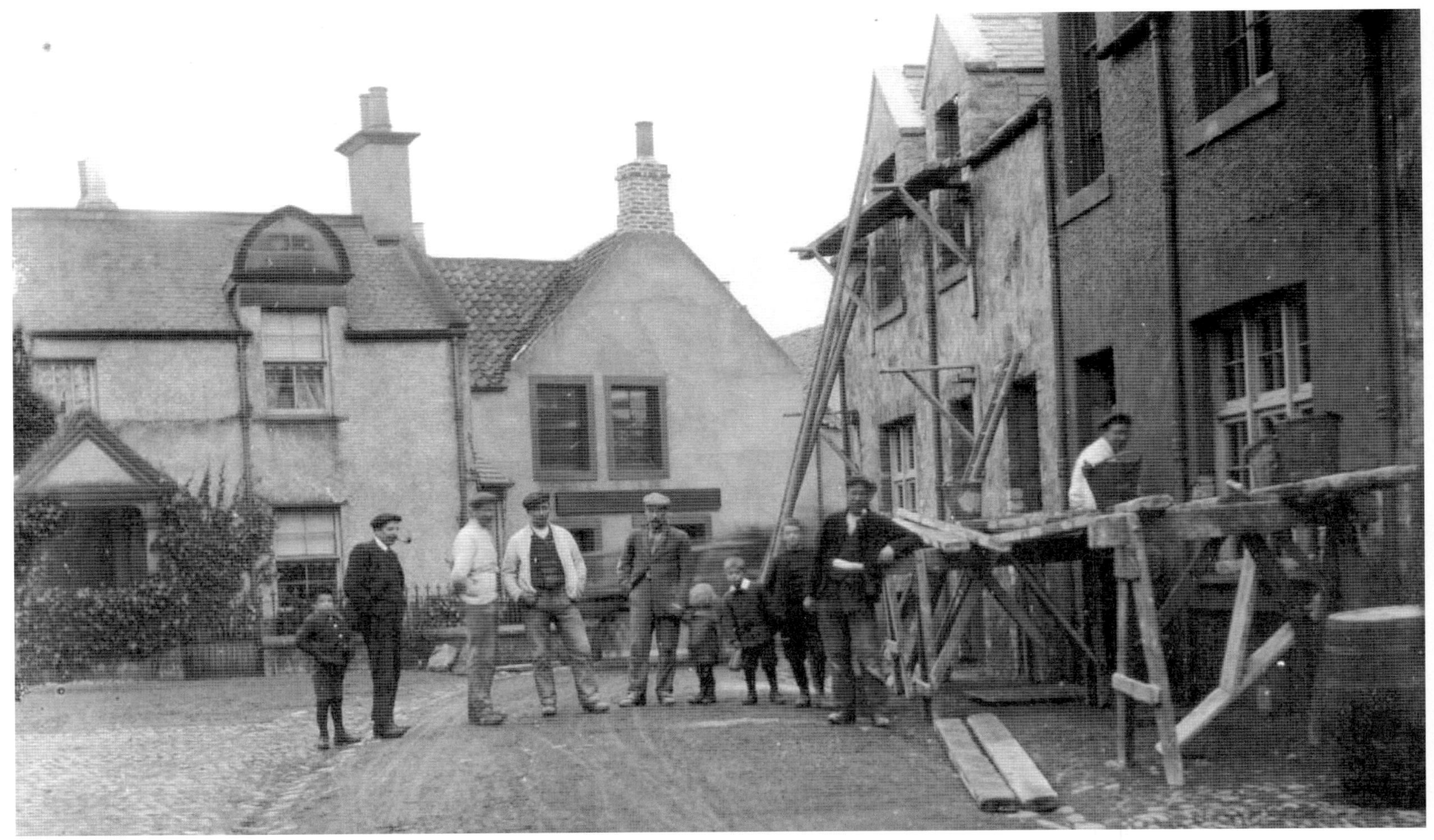

This view looks west towards Coldingham Cross and depicts building work being undertaken in 1907 at the local house known as The Lindens. Local tradesmen seem to be involved in some major renovation work, or even new construction, as the exposed brickwork around the windows and doors is very evident.The house directly in the centre background of the photograph has long since been demolished to make the access road easier for journeying east to St. Abbs. However, there is still a very tight corner and there are numerous 'near-misses' and 'not so near-misses' each year. The photograph was taken by John Wood who also was a master joiner and was employed in this building work.

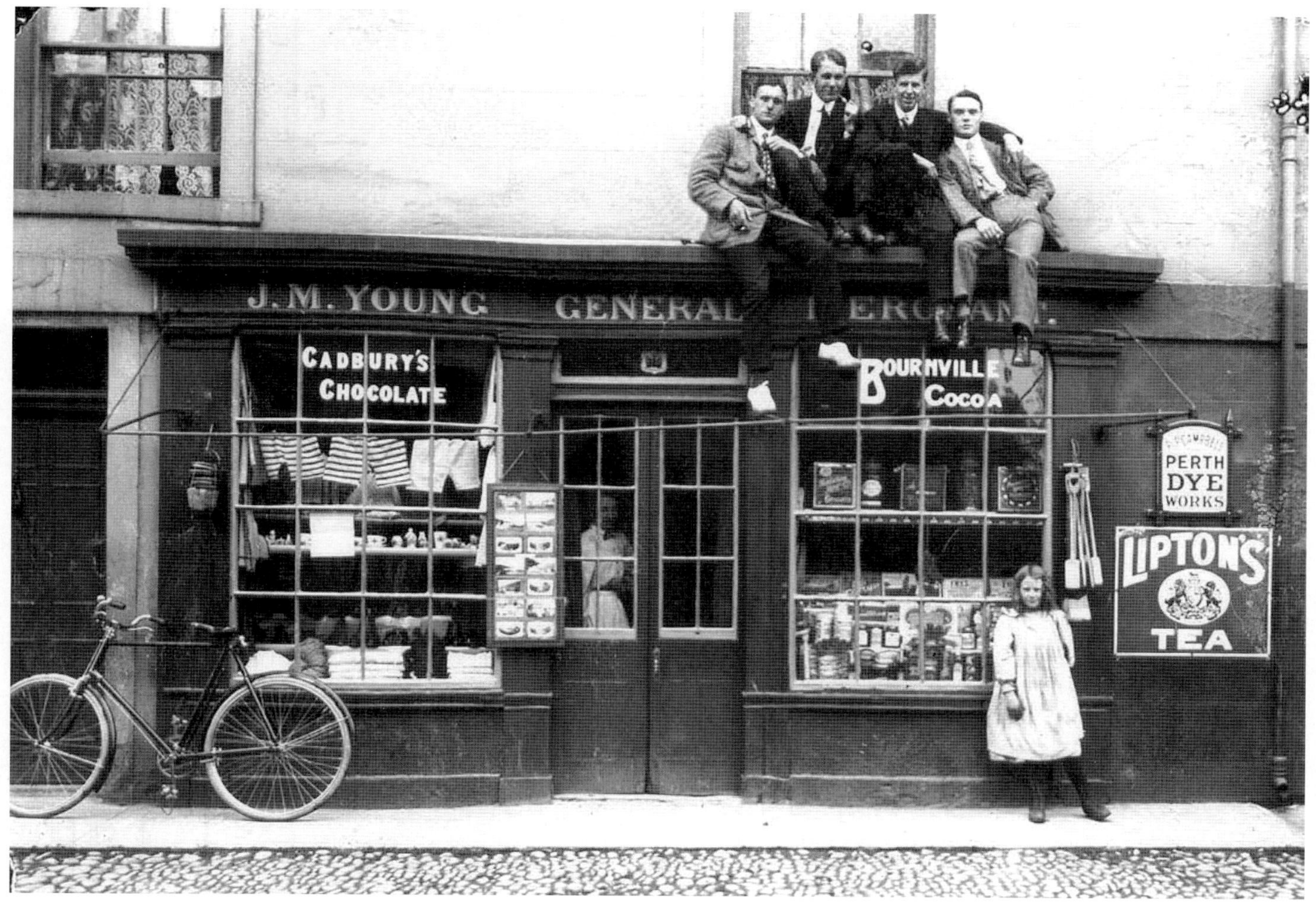

Photographed at the turn of the last century, these four likely lads have climbed above the shop to pose for this photograph. Although their identities are unknown, one can only assume that at least one of them is the owner of the shop, or perhaps the owner's sons. The advertising signage does not help in dating the view and to the left of the doorway, a small display case contains postcards for sale. Whilst this photograph was taken by John Wood, the more commercial postcards would have been taken by the then St. Abbs postmaster Robbie Nisbet.

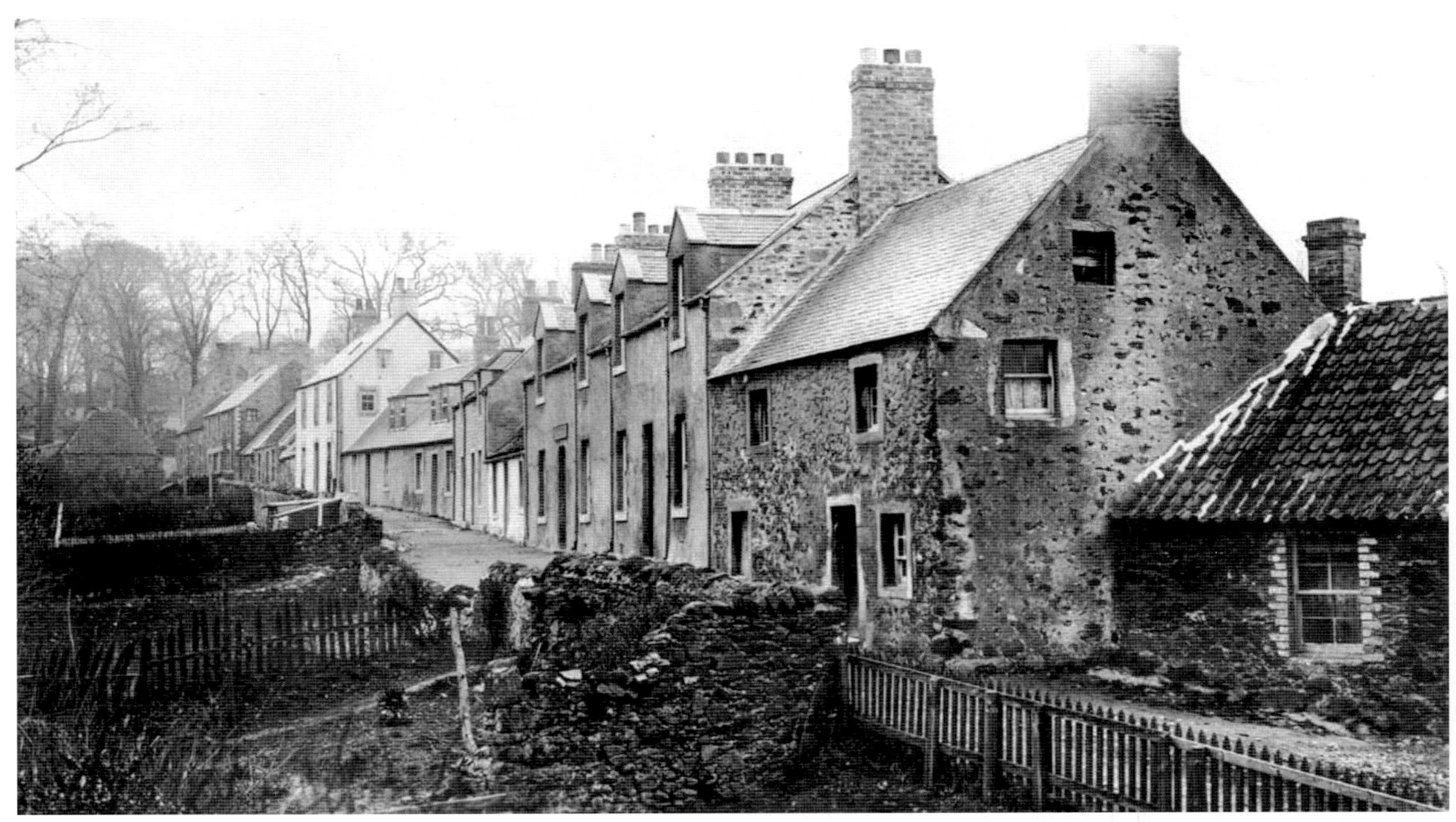

The Bogan. Surprisingly, little has changed of this row of former fishermen's cottages nestled against the burn which runs down the edge of Fishers Brae and onwards to the sea on the other side of the Humbie Knowe at Coldingham Sands. These cottages would have been built either by the fishermen or by the local landowner at the time and feus would have been paid yearly, partly with fish and fish offal, or by the sale of crops or vegetables grown in their allotments. This area of land was originally known as Reckleside or Gosemount Burn, which led into the Court Burn at the bottom of the little valley. There was a large and profitable weaving industry located in the Bogan, but the advent of the American Civil War struck a blow to this local industry from which it never recovered.

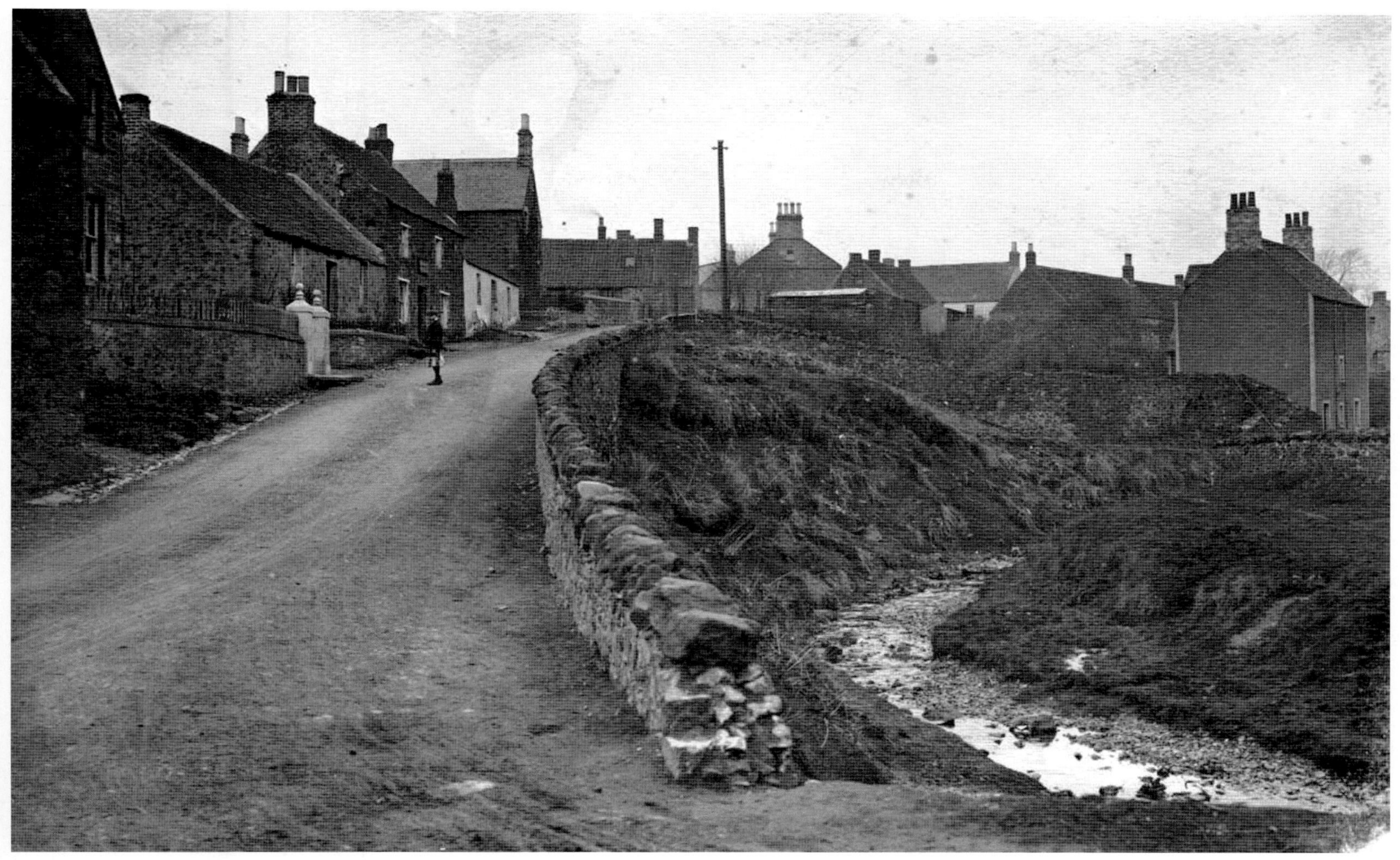

Fishers Brae was the road from Coldingham, leading to the Creel Path and onwards to The Shore. With little or no local transport, the men would walk the couple of miles to the harbour at St. Abbs with their baited hooks and lines carried in 'skulls' across their backs. The small burn which flowed past the Bogan was originally known as Court Burn.

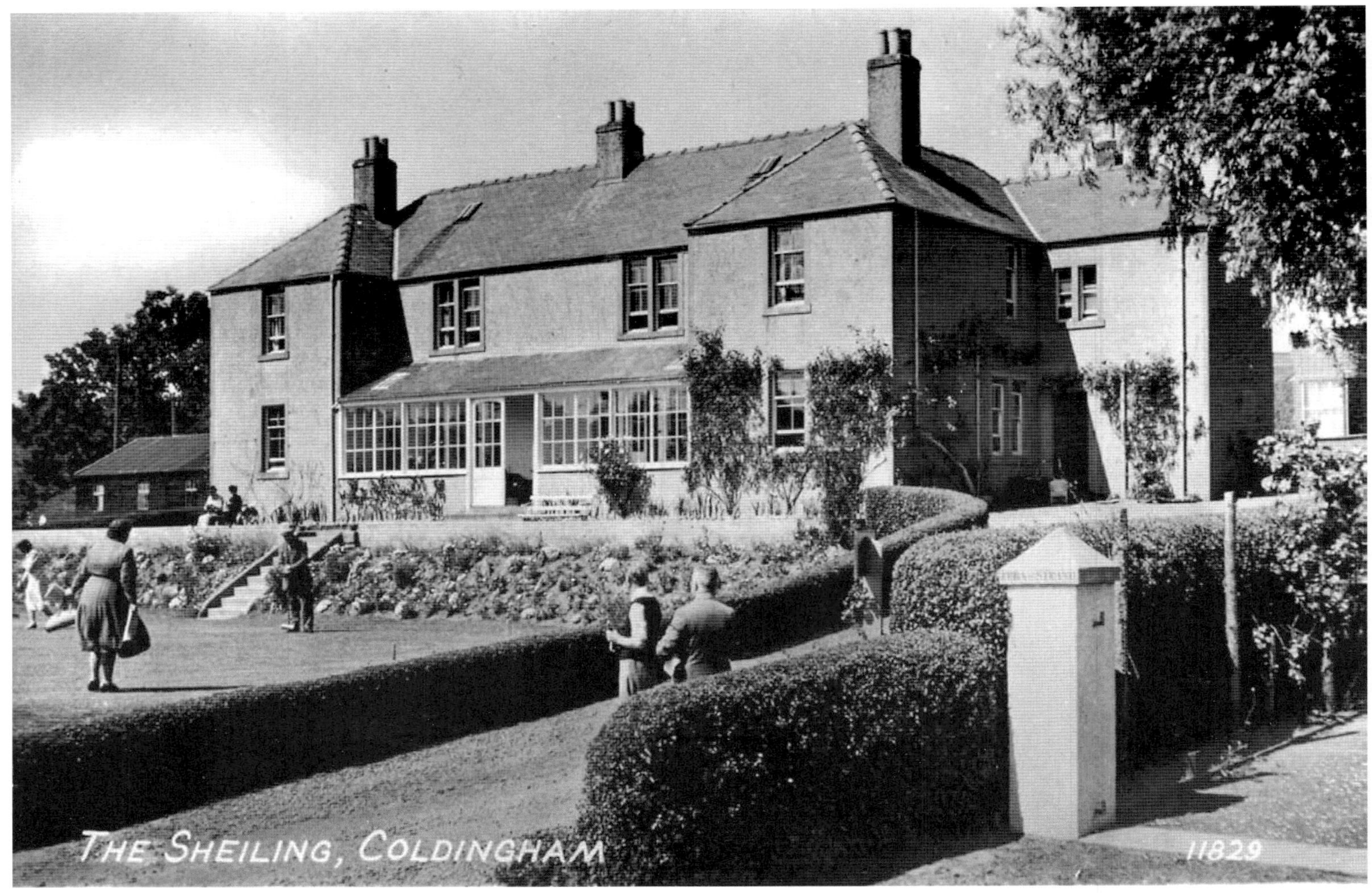

The Shieling is another of those wonderful old buildings built with sensational views in mind as enticement to wealthy travellers to come and enjoy the sea air above Coldingham Sands. Serving as a boarding house and latterly as a retirement home, the building has now been converted into apartments, still with the same unparalleled views of the North Sea.

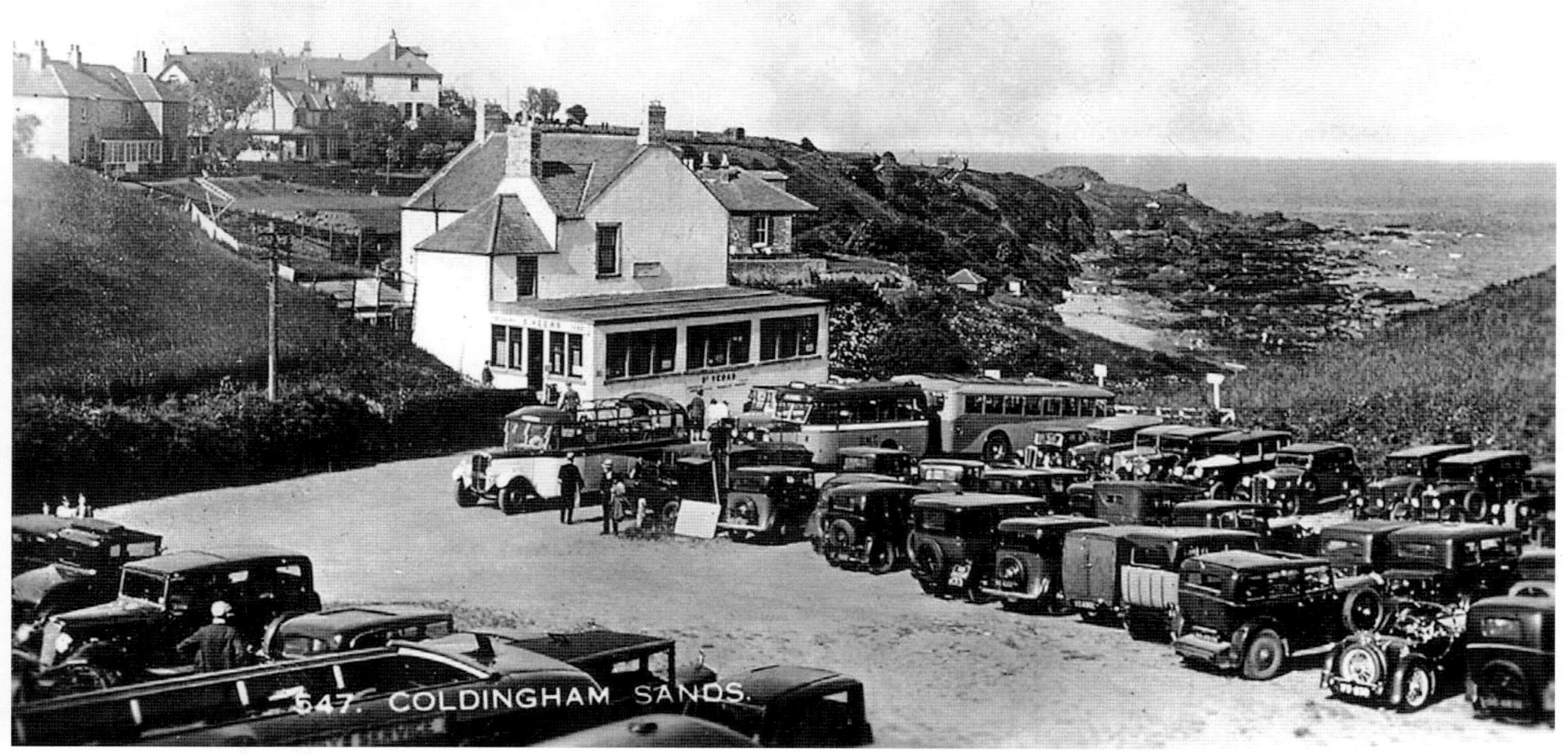

I love this view of the Sands Car Park, with Coldingham Sands at its peak. During the summer months and during special 'Thanksgivings', the car park at the top of the hill leading down to the shore and opposite the St. Vedas Hotel (the building in the foreground) was packed full of cars, buses and charabancs. This must have been a splendid summer's day as there are a couple of convertibles in the car park including a bus which apparently was also able to remove its roof!

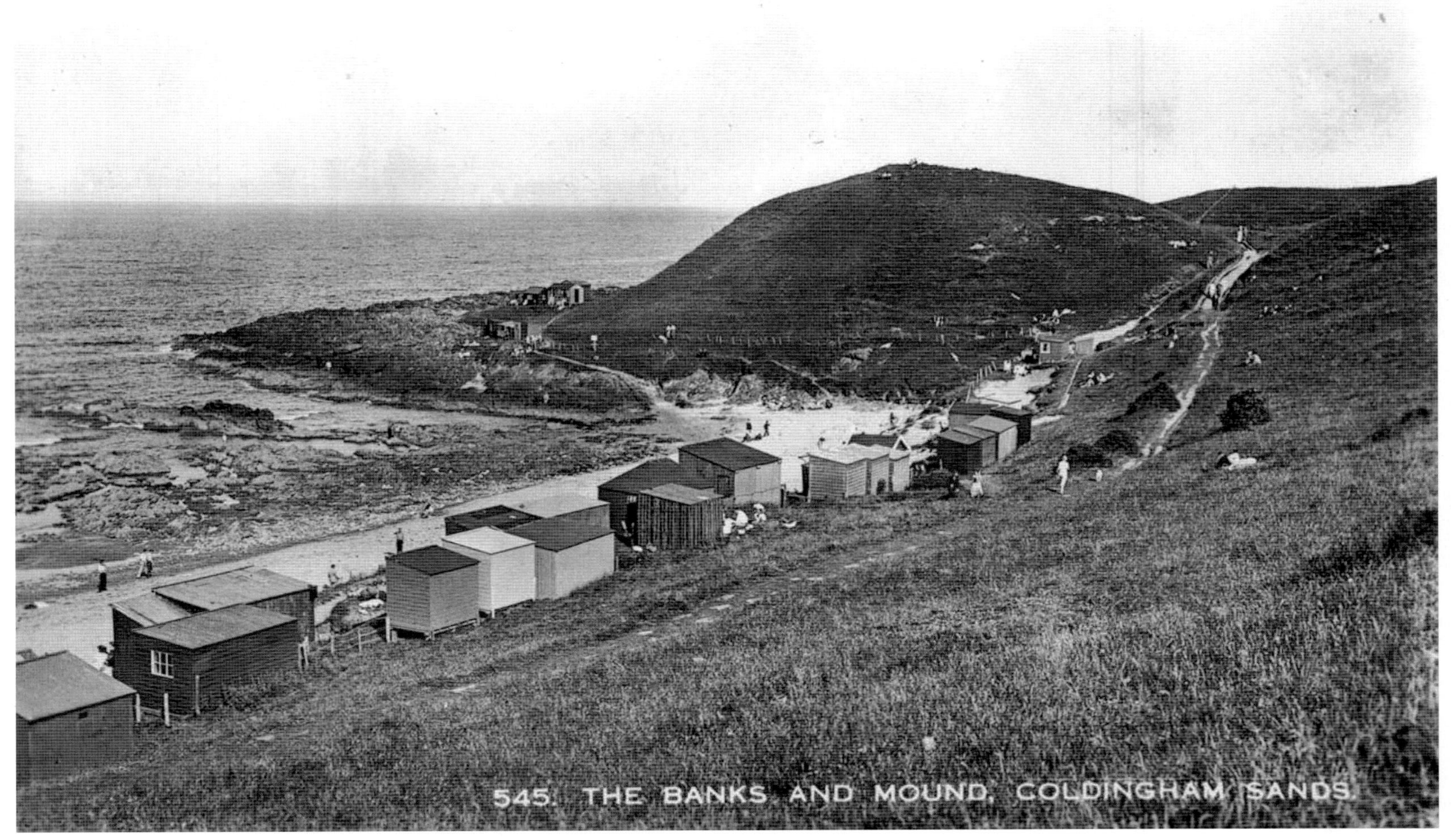

The famous Coldingham Sands, although there is little sand on view on the beach in this picture as it looks like the spring storms have taken much of it away, or deposited it behind the beach huts. Beach huts are very much a British tradition and families have owned these small huts for generations. There are now only around one third of the beach huts that were there previously. The Sands, still very popular in the summer, are now becoming nationally known for surfing.

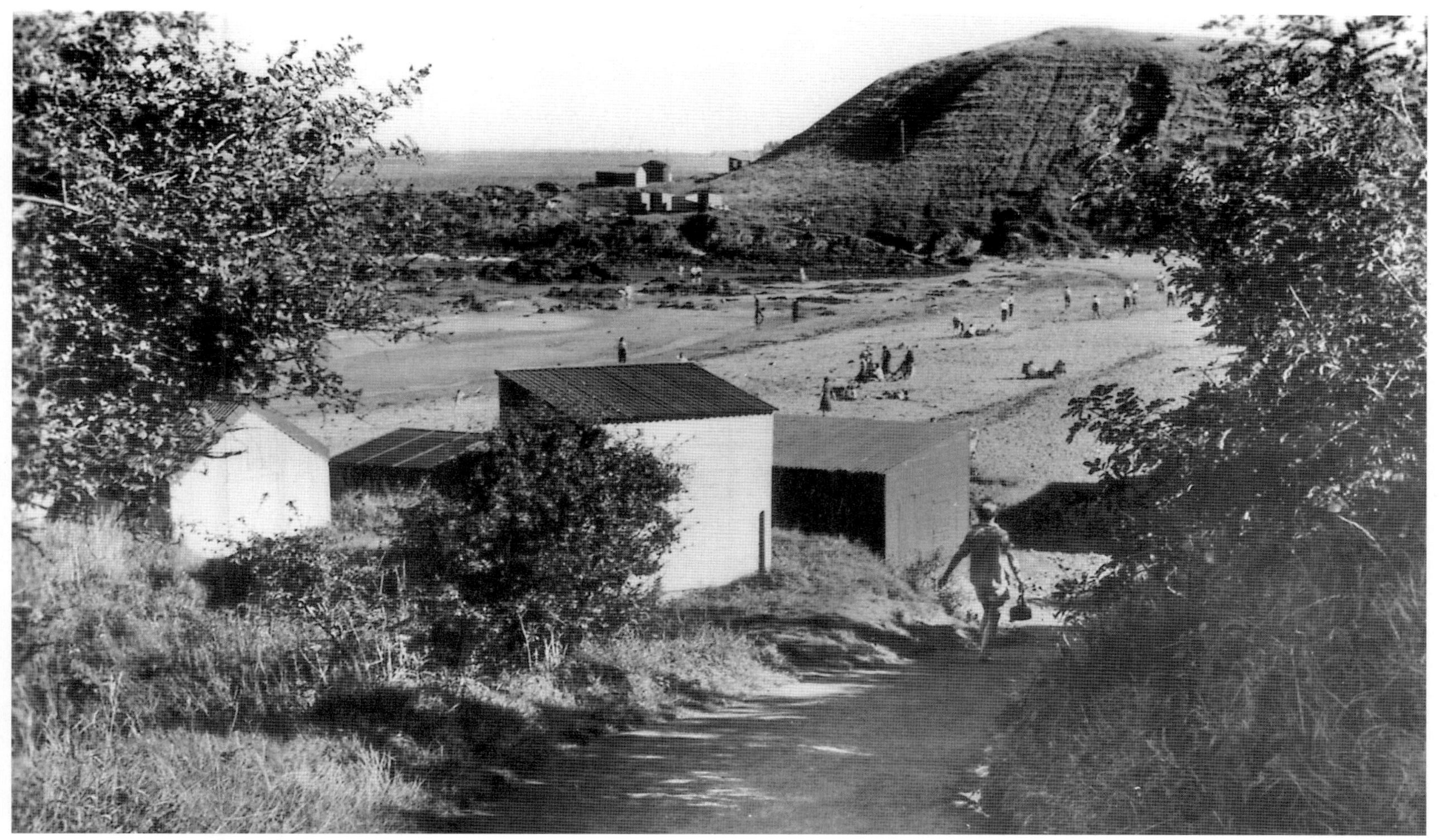

Looking down the brae towards Coldingham Sands and the Humbie Knowe behind. A massive scar on the side of this peculiarly-shaped hillock was the site of an intensive archaeological excavation, in the belief it was perhaps man-made. However, the mound is actually a moraine, pushed down by the ancient glaciers which once stood over two miles thick during the last ice age. Coldingham Bay is an ancient volcanic crater and there is a ridge of rock out to sea which forms part of the outer rim.

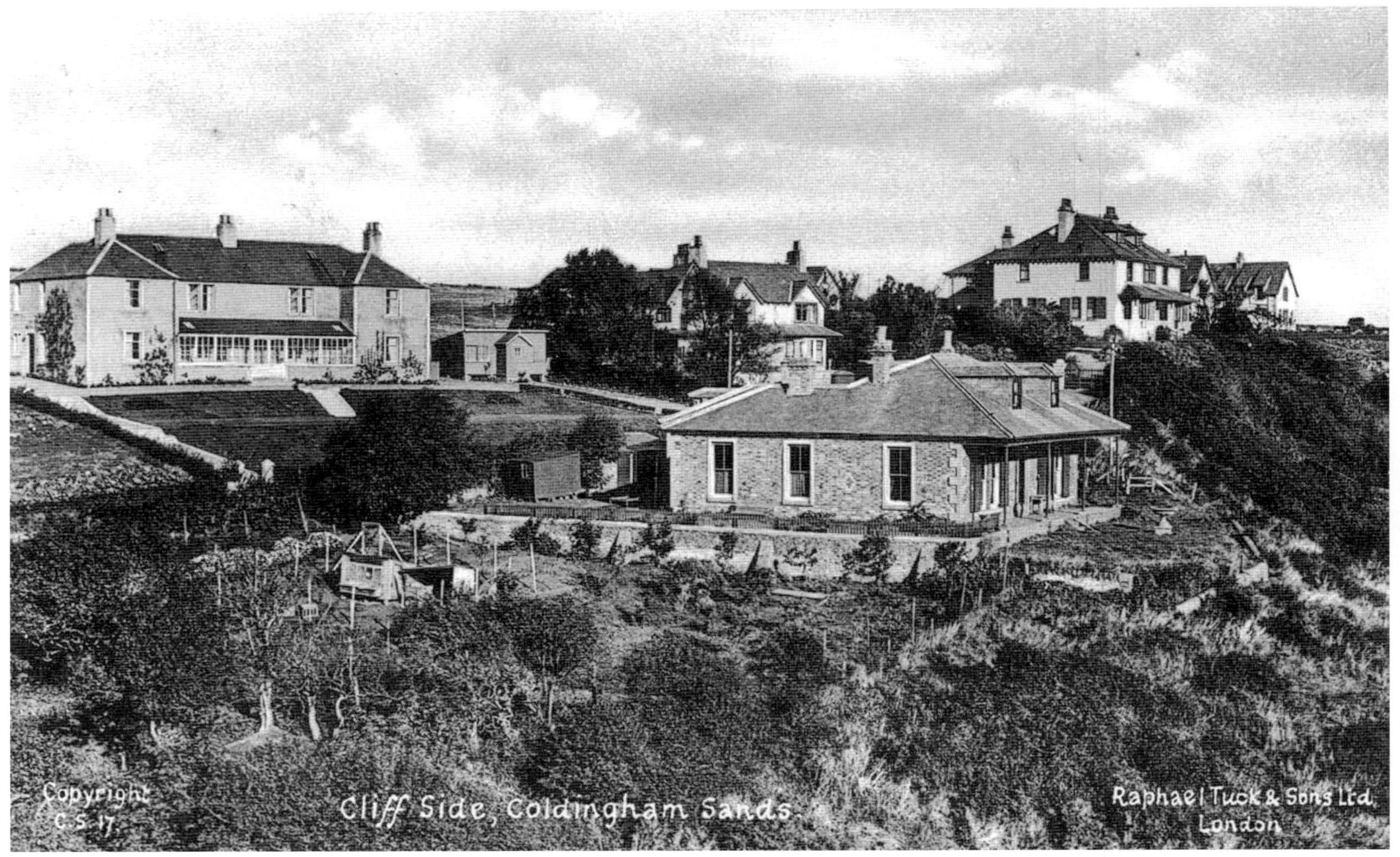

The first of the private homes to be built along what was known as the Lea Banks or Sea Banks, depending on whose history you are reading was Sea Neuk which still stands today just before you walk down the brae to the sands. An elegant house, it is quite prominent and a further handful of large homes followed, including the St.Vedas Hotel, The Shieling, The Haven and Dunlaverock.

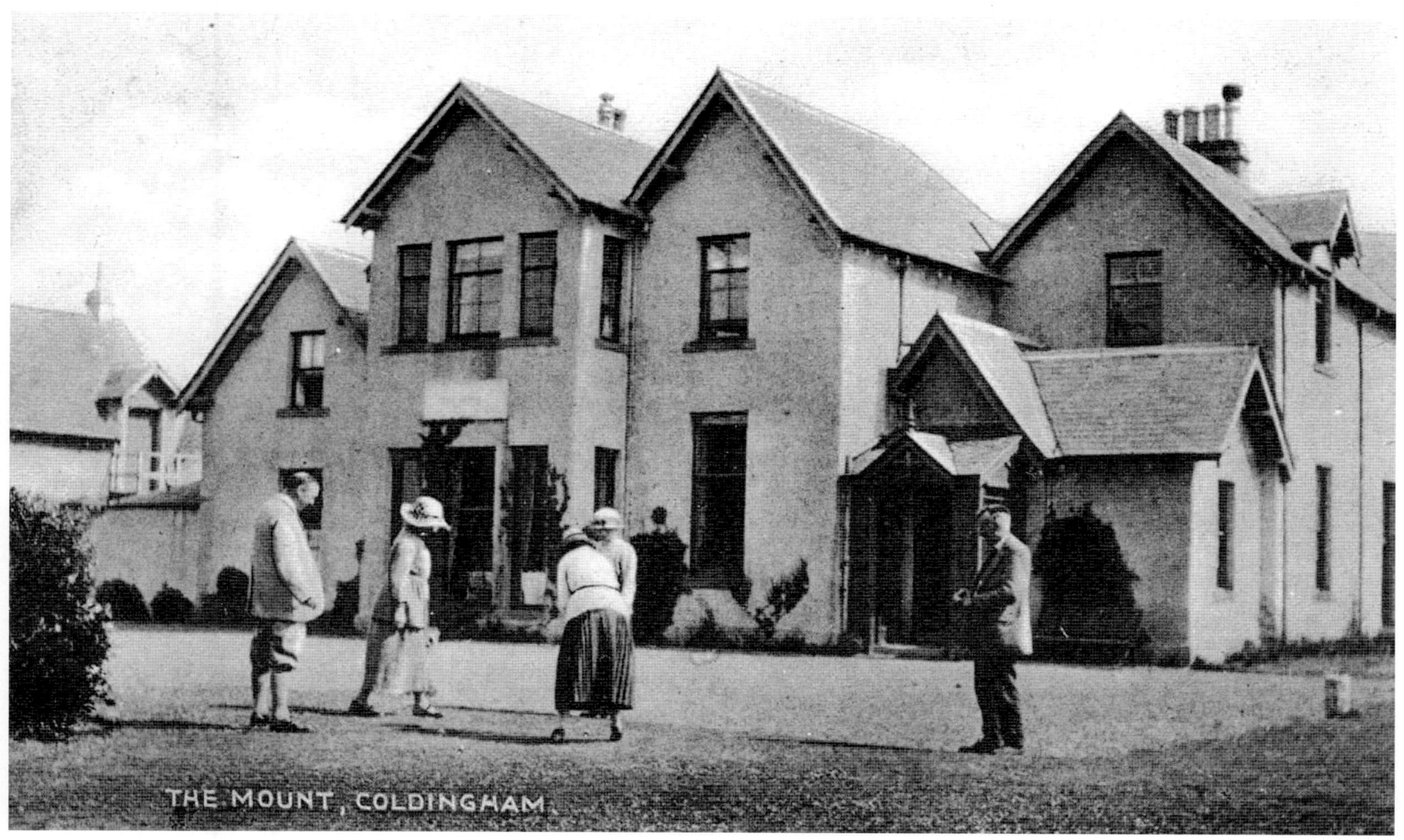

The Mount, overlooking Coldingham Sands and the Humbie Knowe, has had a variety of uses. Originating as a private residence, it sought favour as a private hotel, before becoming a hospital for injured soldiers during World War I and then serving as a convalescent home for many years after. It then continued as a guest house, before housing the military during World War II and afterwards becoming one of the leading Youth Hostel Association's buildings in Scotland. Now it is entering a new era and the building is for sale. Who knows what the next phase in her grand life will be?

The St. Abbs Haven Hotel with her protective Home Guard during World War I. Originally built by Isabelle Cowe, famously it was used by Isabelle and her sisters who looked after the children orphaned after the sinking of the Titanic on 15th April 1912. The Haven gained in popularity and began to take paying guests who enjoyed her luxurious gardens and splendid views. Another building was constructed half way down the hill towards Coldingham Sands and this housed the dozens of staff who were once employed there. It was expanded over the years, losing much of its character, and is now subdivided into private apartments.

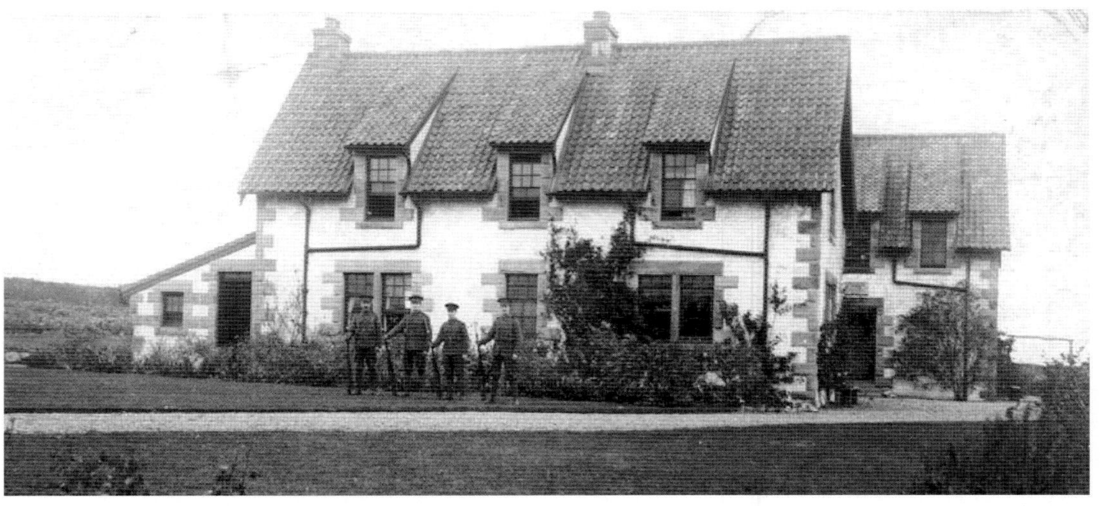

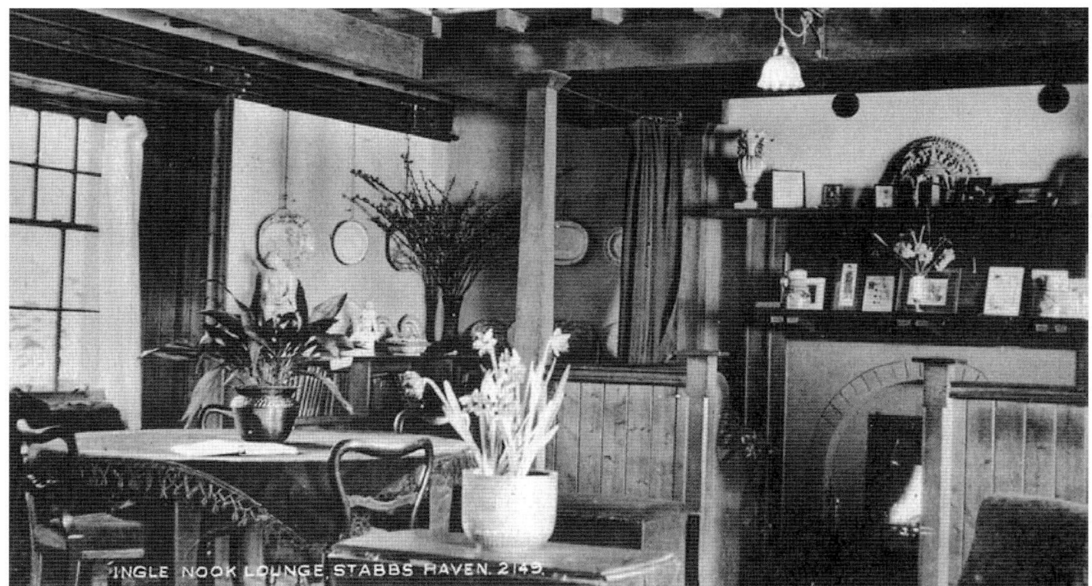

One of the early views of The Haven during her classic Victorian splendour with the ubiquitous aspidistra plant on the table, fine wood panelling, a cosy seating area around the natural fire and this drawing room, overlooked by an open gallery with beautiful woodwork and fine paintings, including one of St. Ebba, who is said to still haunt the property. This fine old building is another which has been converted into rather expensive holiday apartments.

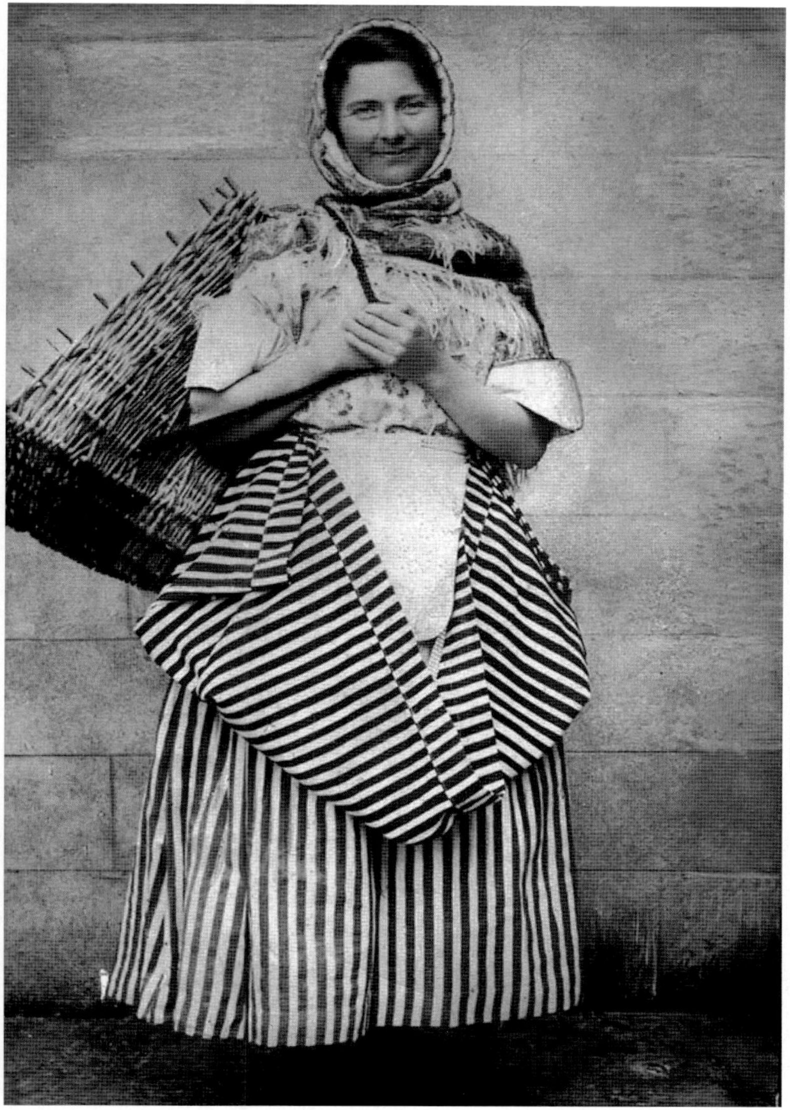

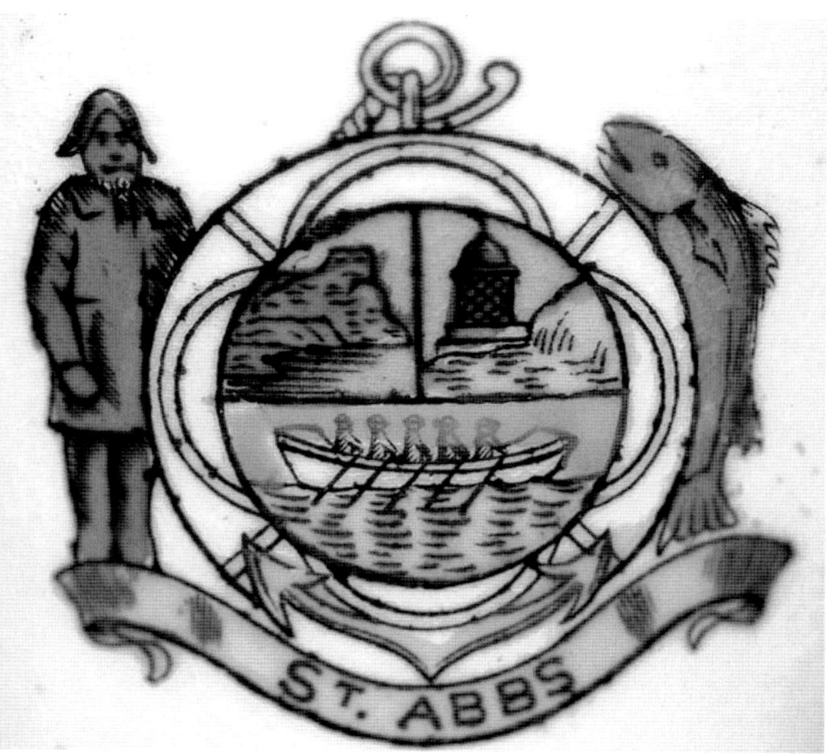

Isabelle Cowe (after St. Ebba) was probably one of the most celebrated women from St. Abbs. A beautiful woman in every sense of the word, seen here in the traditional fish wife's clothing, she was photographed many times. Isabelle and her sisters were responsible for The Haven. The coat of arms is another matter; there is no original artwork of this and the illustration comes from a piece of highly collectable ornamental pottery believed to have been produced by Robbie Nisbet, the sub-postmaster of St. Abbs. It is very symbolic in nature with the fisherman, herring, the first lifeboat, a prominent rock known as Jock's Nose and the original lighthouse. It is hoped that a more modern representation will be made of this heraldry and used as a symbol for the village.

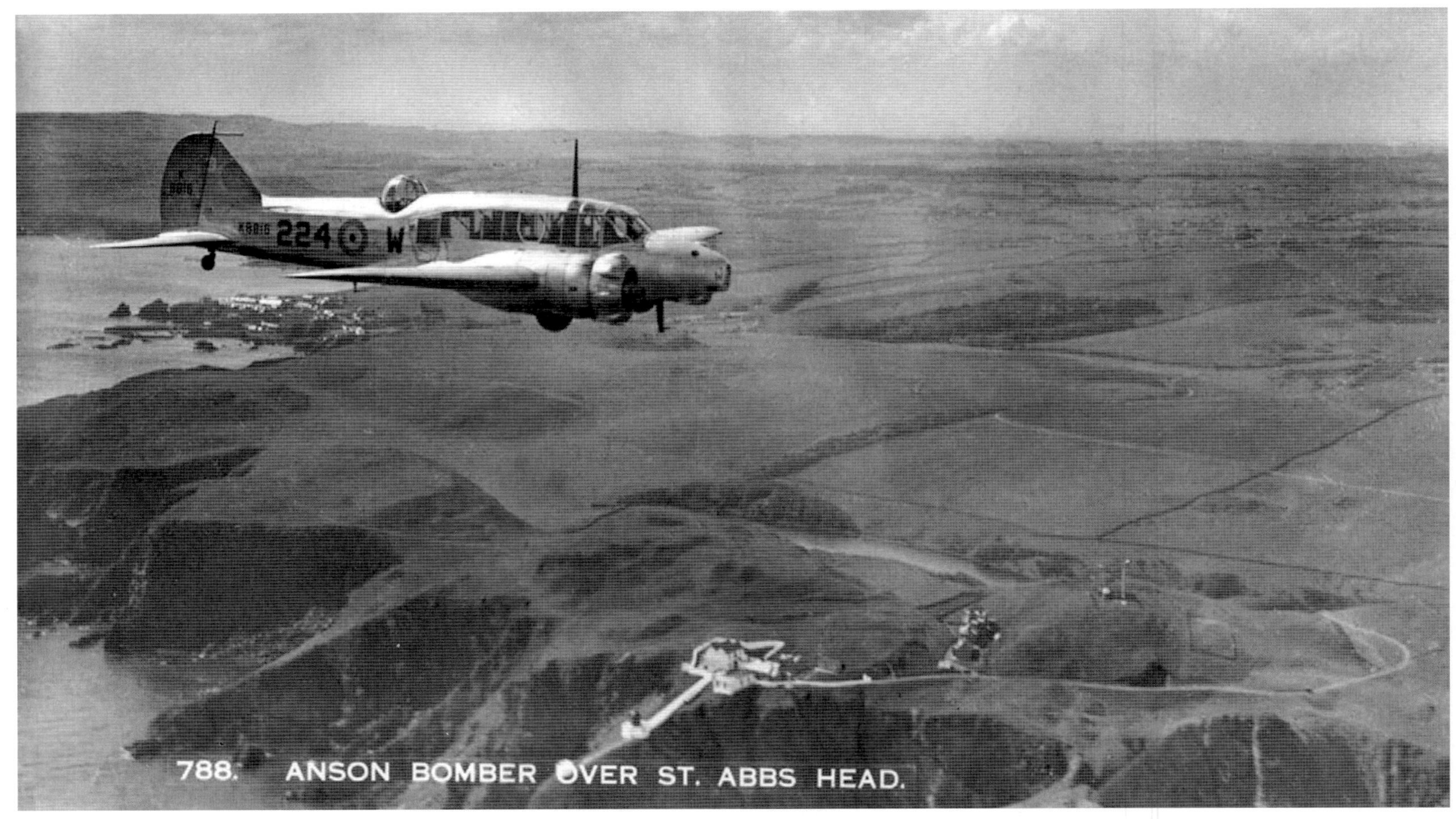

This unusual aerial view was quite clearly taken by another aircraft, probably another Avro Anson Bomber. Known amongst pilots as 'Faithful Annie' these bombers were described as slow, cold and noisy, but actually became the most famous British aircrew trainer of all time. The Anson Bomber first flew on 24 March 1935 and was originally used for maritime reconnaissance, although it proved unsuitable and was mothballed. However, as it was the first RAF monoplane with a retractable undercarriage, it saw new life as a trainer with over 11,000 aeroplanes built until it ceased production in 1952. Here, one of the aeroplanes is flying over St. Abbs Head with the lighthouse clearly on view. Northfield Farm stretches away in the background and the village of St. Abbs is just visible on the coast.

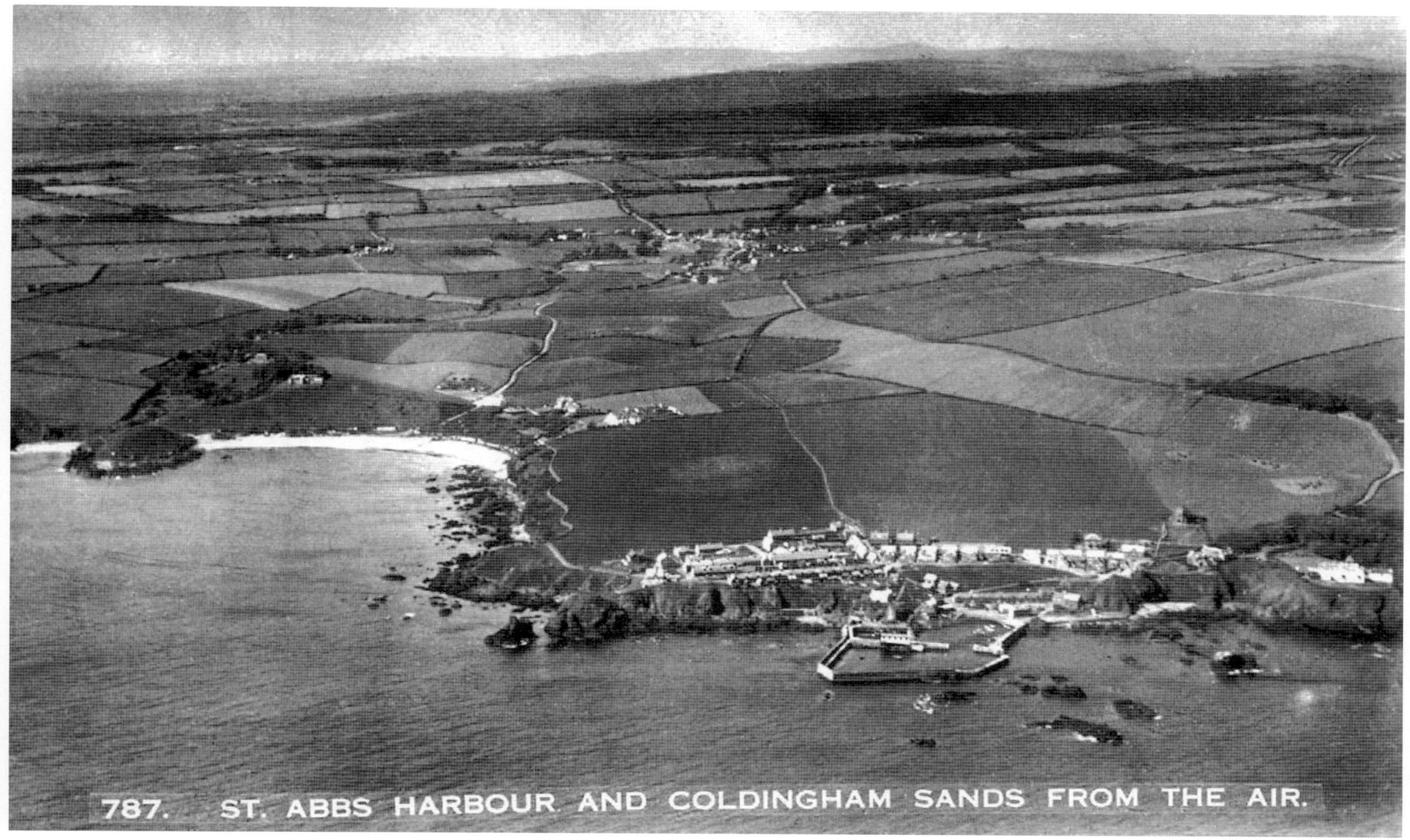

This aerial view of St. Abbs village and harbour has changed little over the years. Apart from a few more houses, the harbour has not changed at all in the last 100 years or so. Photographed from an Avro Anson Bomber on a commercial flight up the coast, it is known that this 'photo-shoot' certainly covered Seahouses, Holy Island, Berwick upon Tweed, Eyemouth, St. Abbs, Dunbar and North Berwick. The wide stretch of white is Coldingham Sands and Milldown Beach is further to the left.

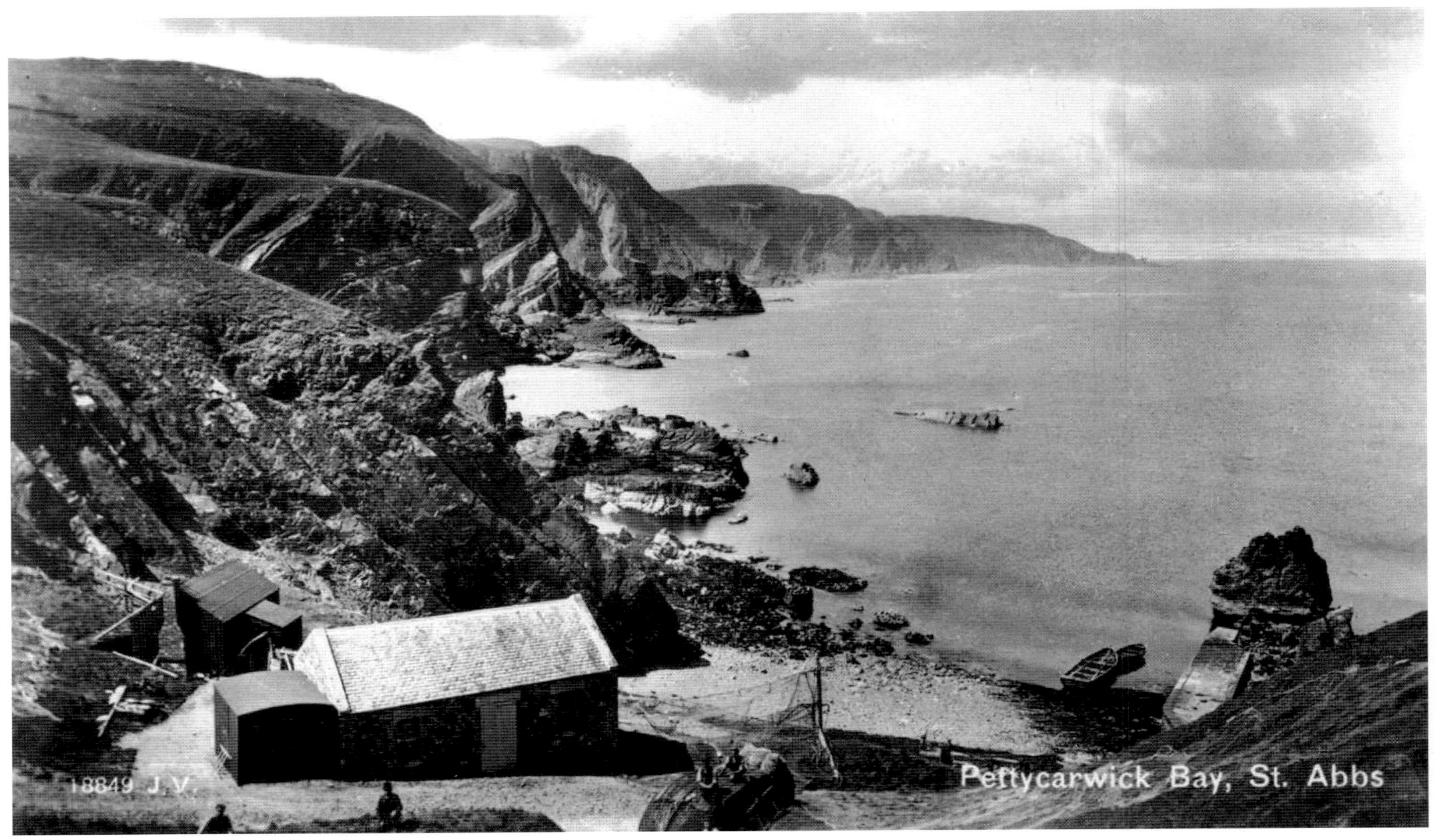

Petty Carr Wick Bay gradually changed its name to Petticowick Bay over the years and at one time hosted a very successful salmon fishing station. Whilst St. Abbs can hardly be seen as being near the mouth of the famous River Tweed, twelve miles to the south, the waters in this stretch of the coastline held vast quantities of salmon at one time and in fact were so plentiful, that they were seen as food for the poor or even to feed livestock. Here quite a sturdy house can be seen with a variety of storage sheds around, one boat upturned next to the house, another in the water and nets hanging up to dry. The slipway was installed by the Northern Lighthouse Board.

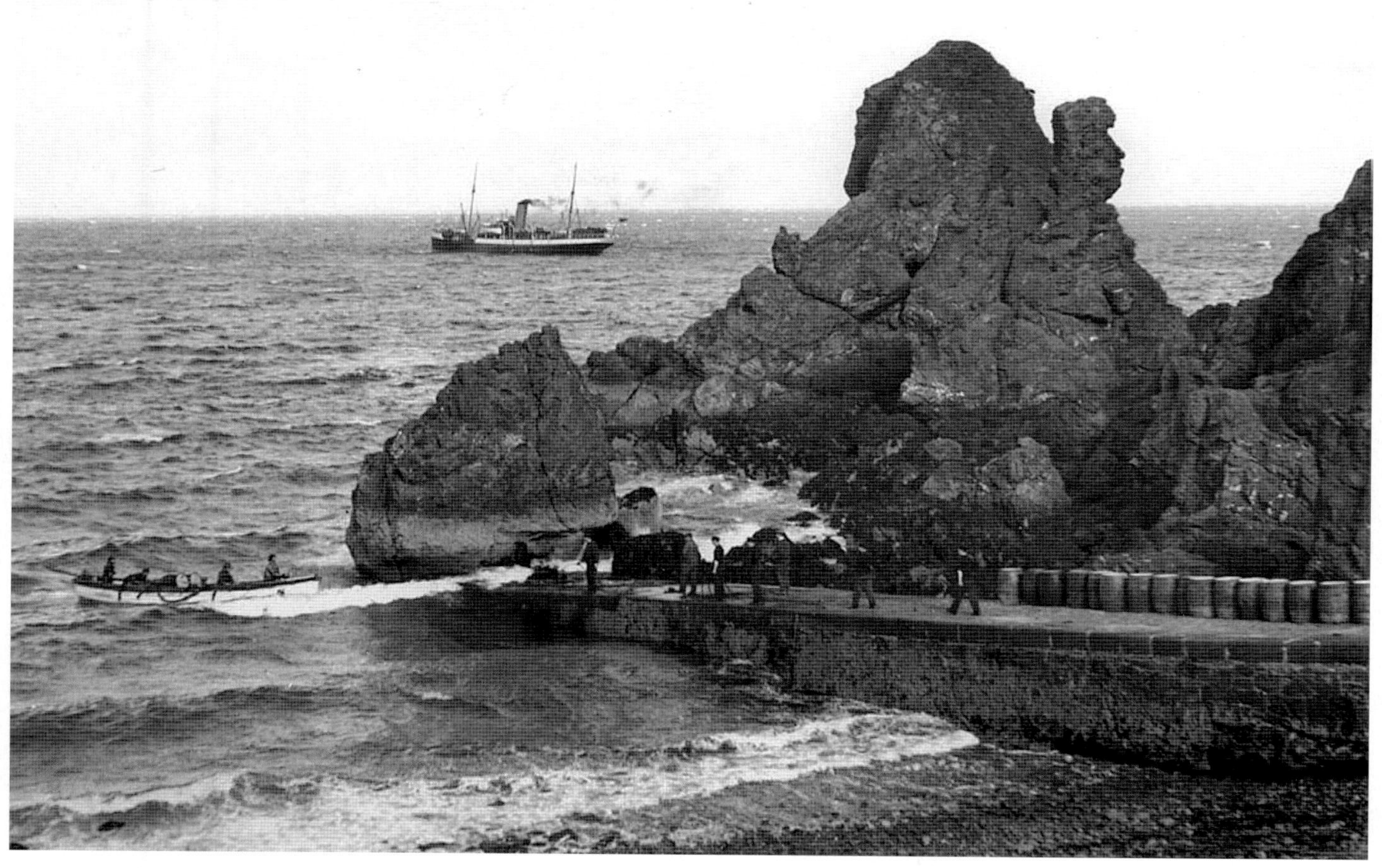

This slipway was indeed the only access for stores and supplies to be made available for the St. Abbs Lighthouse, as the road from St. Abbs was not constructed until many years later, as motor transport became more popular. The slipway is stacked with barrels and the supply ship's tender is negotiating the choppy swell as it approaches the slipway. The ship in this photograph was the Leith based *Pharos IV*. A steel twin-screw steamer, built in 1909, by William Beardmore & Co Ltd, Glasgow, Yard No. 496. At 921 gross tons, she was 206ft long. She was finally scrapped in Charlestown, Fife in 1955 after having been renamed *Avontoun*, in order to release the name for the next more modern version of the Northern Lighthouse Board's supply ships. There have been ten ships with the name Pharos since 1799.

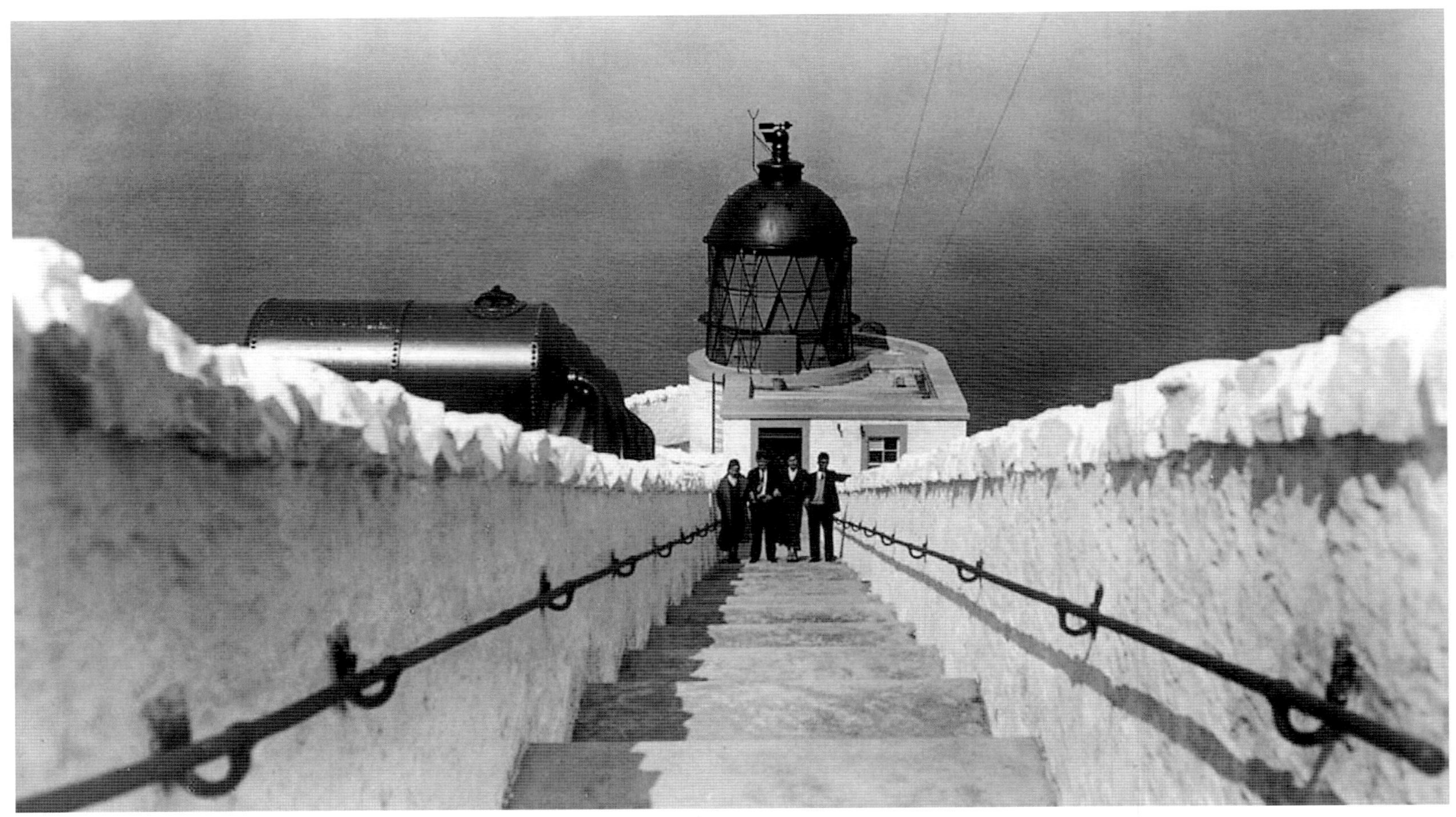

After the sinking of the *Martello* on Carr Rock in 1857, the Northern Lighthouse Board recommended the erection of a lighthouse at St. Abbs Head to assist in navigation. The lighthouse, designed and built by David and Thomas Stevenson, was completed in 1862, the oil burning lamp first being exhibited on the 24th of February of that year. This was changed to an incandescent lamp in 1906 and an electrically operated one in 1966. In 1876 St. Abbs was the first lighthouse in Scotland to be installed with the siren fog signal, driven by hot air engines. Oil replaced this in 1911 and diesel-powered engines replaced these in December 1955. The fog signal was discontinued in 1987. The lighthouse's elevation is 68 metres above the sea and it can be nominally seen over 40 kilometres away.

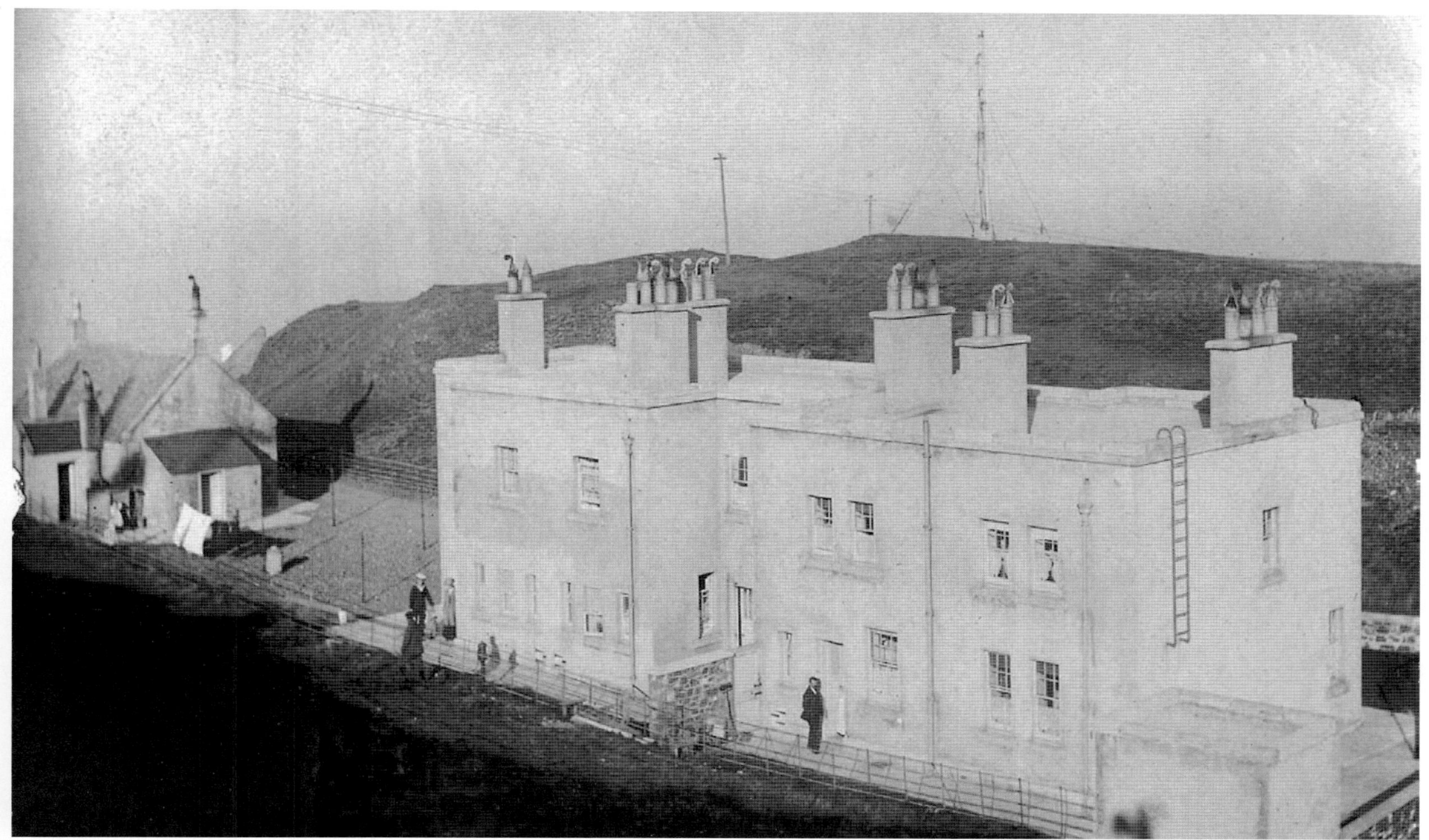

The former St. Abbs Lighthouse staff were stationed in a rather splendid group of buildings near to the lighthouse, a little more sheltered from the ravages of the east coast weather. Amongst cliffs teeming with seabirds in one of Britain's most important National Nature Reserves, the lighthouse-keepers led a rather privileged (although rather lonely) life. These grand buildings were demolished at the turn of the last century in favour of new houses and offices much closer to the light. The lighthouse became automated in 1993 and the more modern buildings were sold off as private dwelling houses.

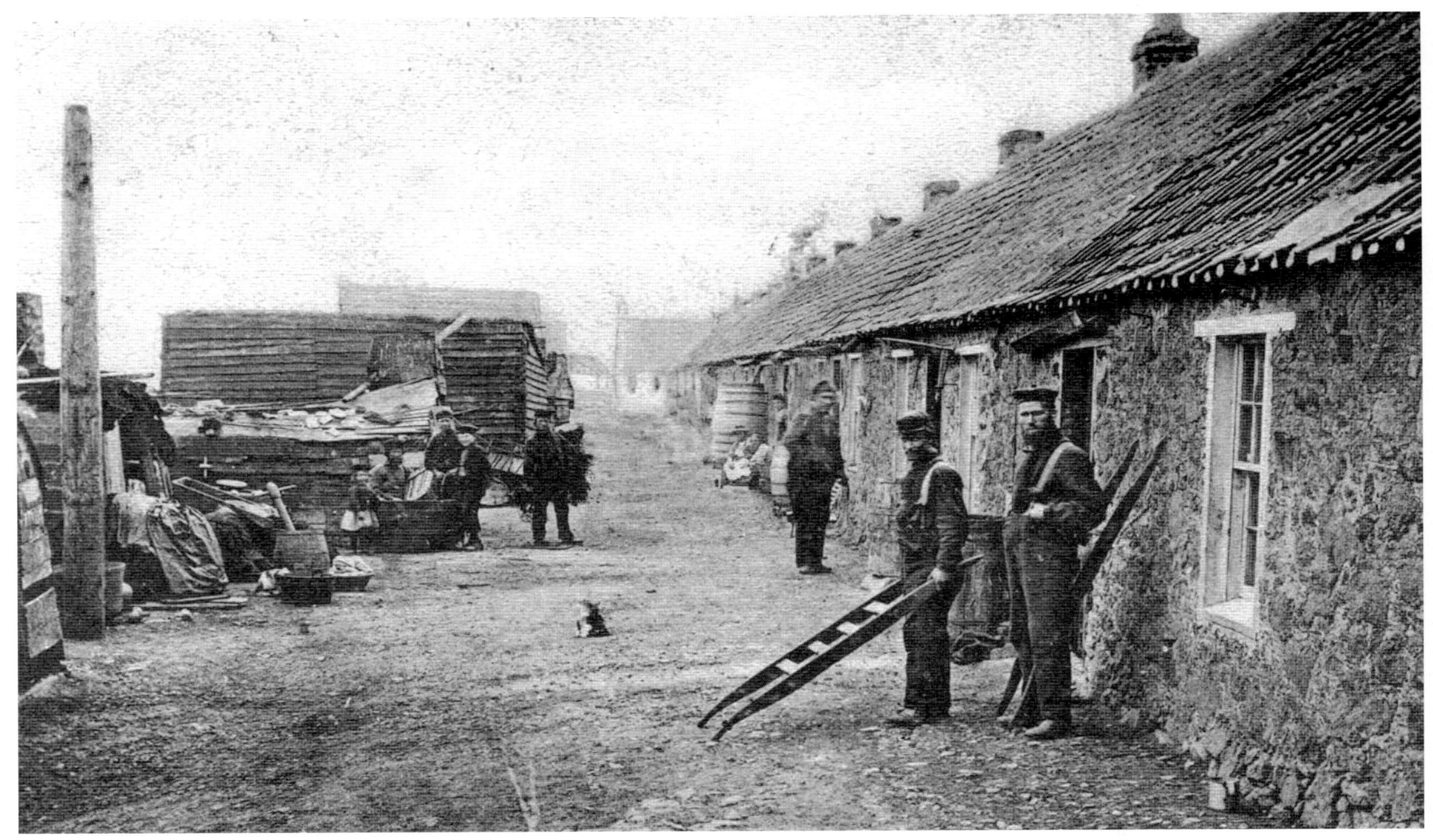

Seaview Terrace was originally known as the Upper Row and was located at the top of the hill overlooking the harbour. Upper Row and Under Row (see page 43) were built in the late 18th century as the principal residences of the early St. Abbs families. They were originally constructed of clat and clay and had an earthen floor, and a simple fire and grate. The tenants were expected to pay for all the internal walls and ceilings and the cost was not reimbursed if they left. The wooden sheds on the seaward side of the houses were made from the hulls of upturned fishing boats. The stretcher apparatus was used to carry the heavy hemp ropes and nets from the stores to the harbour.

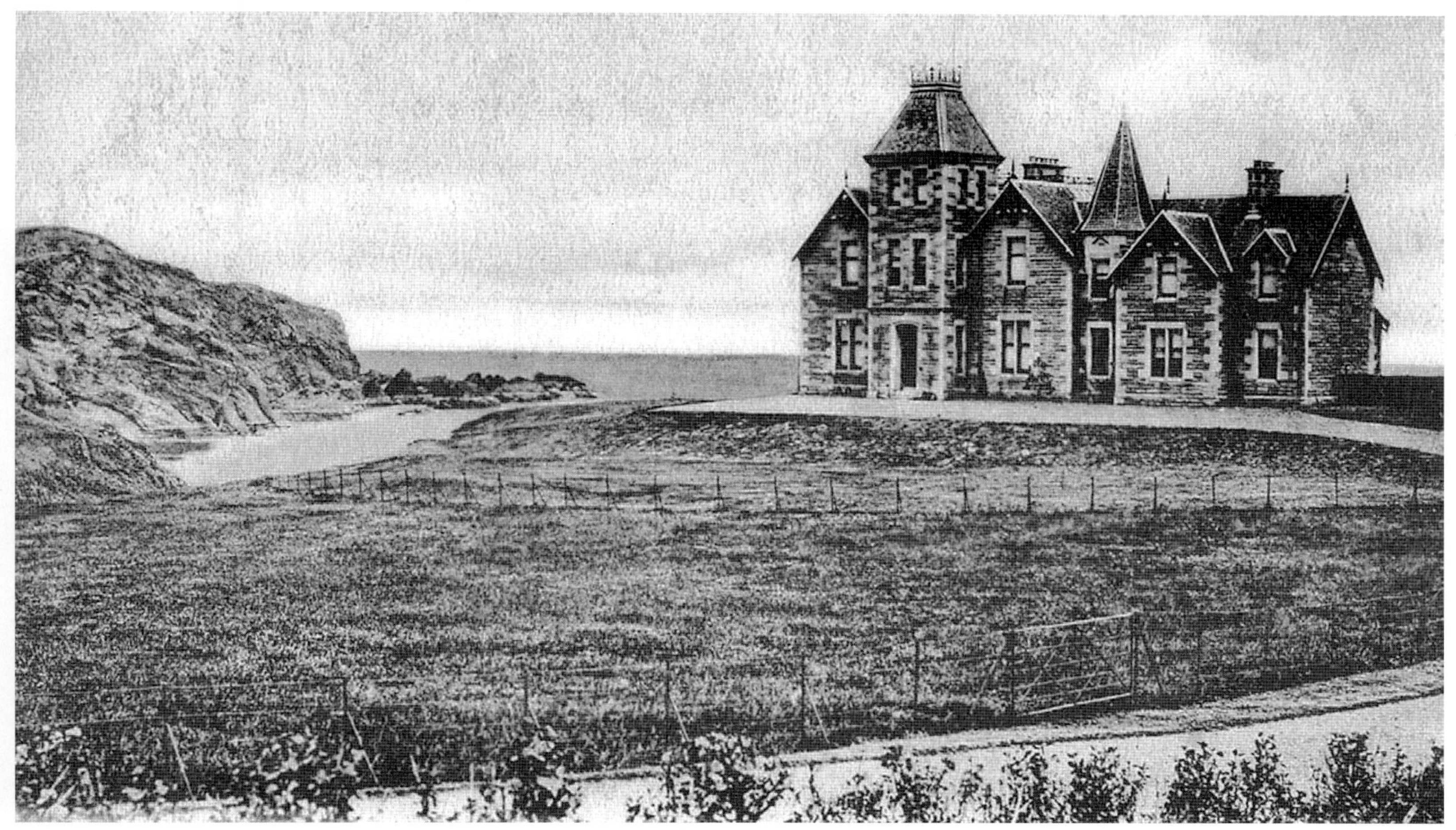

One of the earliest views of Northfield House, traditional home of the Lord of the Manor. This mansion was built by Henry Home Drummond Esq. who then let the property to Mr. Brodie. The present Northfield House has seen many changes, particularly from a structural perspective. The current owners have just completed a massive refurbishment of one of the most strategically placed mansions in the British Isles. Mr & Mrs Nisbet and their family are worthy benefactors of the town and stewards of what is now, a superb family home.

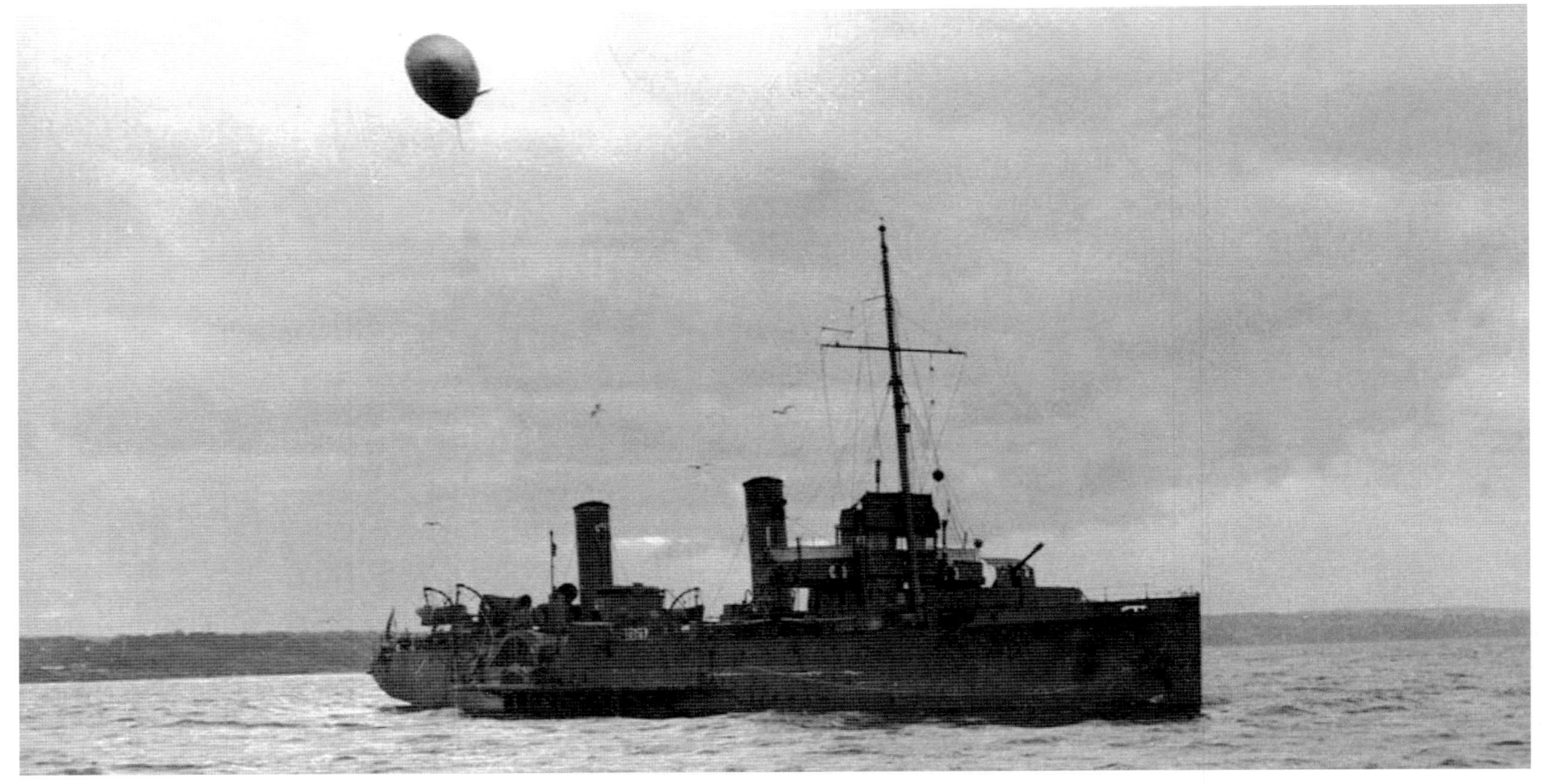

The author Aldous Huxley was staying in Northfield House when *HMS Pathfinder* blew up on September 5th 1914. *HMS Pathfinder* was built by Cammell Laird, laid down August 1903 and completed in July 1905. One of a pair of boats in the Pathfinder Class, she had only a partial armoured deck with side armour covering the engine rooms rather than the more usual full length protective deck. *HMS Pathfinder* was originally to have been named *Fastnet* but the name was changed before construction began. She was capable of speeds in excess of 25 knots and was 379 feet in length. Armed with 10 x 12 pounder QF (10 x 1); 8 x 3 pounder QF (8 x 1) and 2 x 18in TT guns she was thought to be speedy and dangerous, but on September 5th 1914 she became the first British warship to be attacked by submarine and sunk by torpedo, by the U-21, commanded by Leutnant zur See Otto Hersing. On this day *HMS Pathfinder* was only capable of achieving 5 knots in speed due to a shortage of coal and the submarine had an easy picking. The torpedo struck the main magazine, which blew the ship to smithereens, just east of St. Abbs Head Lighthouse. 259 lost their lives that day; the St. Abbs lifeboat assisted in rescuing just eleven survivors.

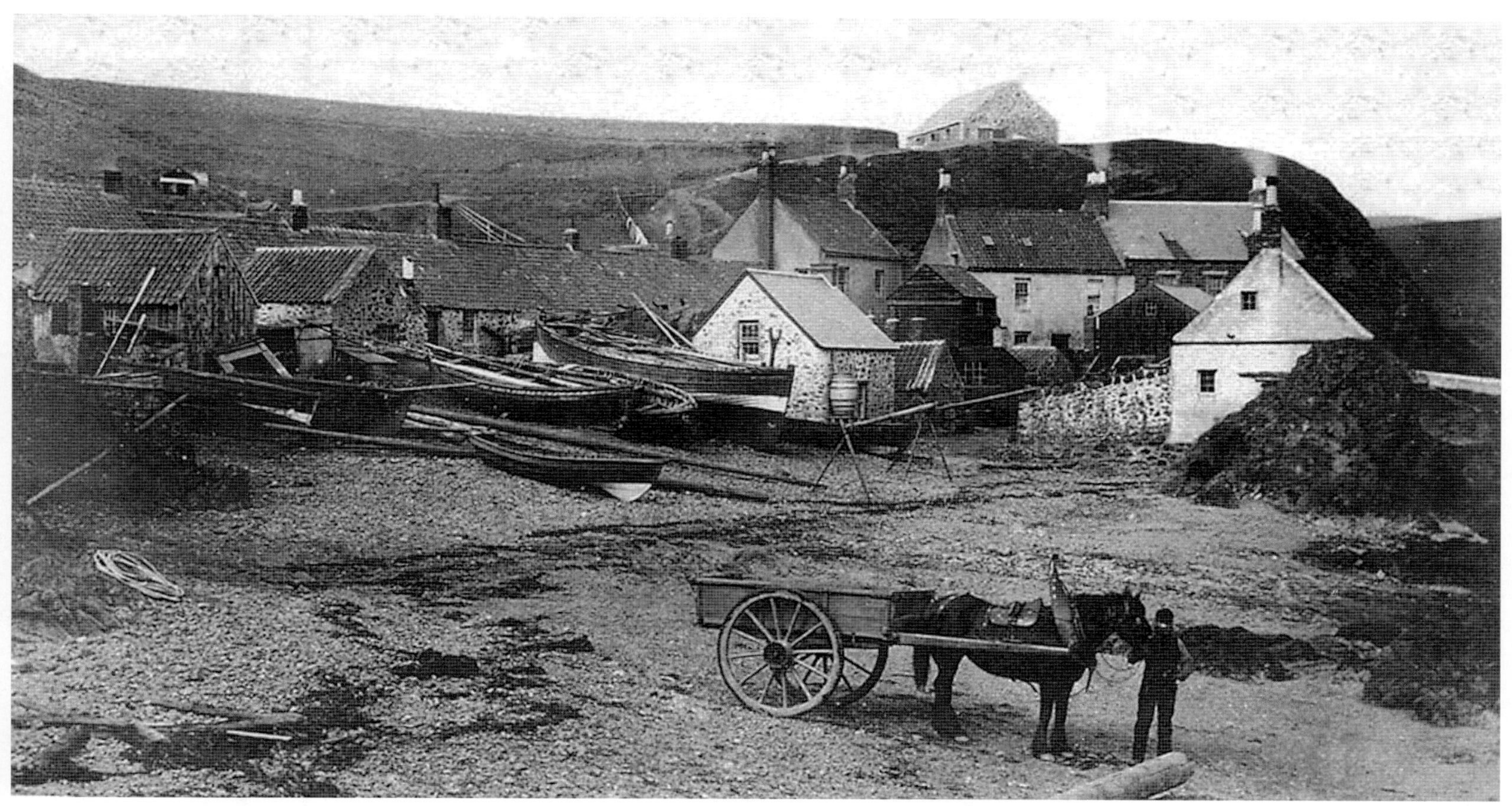

This is perhaps the earliest photograph of St. Abbs village, taken before the outer harbour was built in 1890. The original harbour was built in 1833 at what was then known as 'Northfield Shore' as Northfield and the farm estate owned all of the surrounding land. The village which grew up around the harbour and her sixteen boats at the time became known as Coldingham Shore, as many of the fishermen lived in Coldingham. In this view the village hall can be seen at the top of the hill, but there are no other houses to be seen along what is now Briery Law. The village hall was opened in 1860 and was also the school and the church, until the new church was built and opened in 1892. The school was opened in 1887. The photo also shows the original Rock House which was destroyed during a massive storm. Quite clearly there is no harbour as such and the fishing boats have been hauled up the beach over logs, used as rollers. In extreme tidal conditions, these houses and fish curing sheds were at the mercy of the waves. Under Row is established, as are quite a few other buildings in the background. Today most have gone. Even Rock House is completely changed.

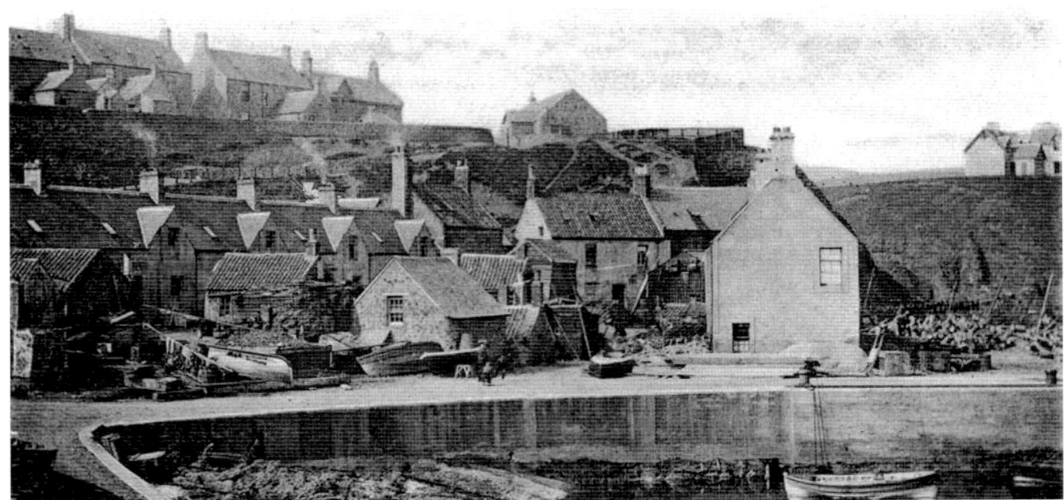

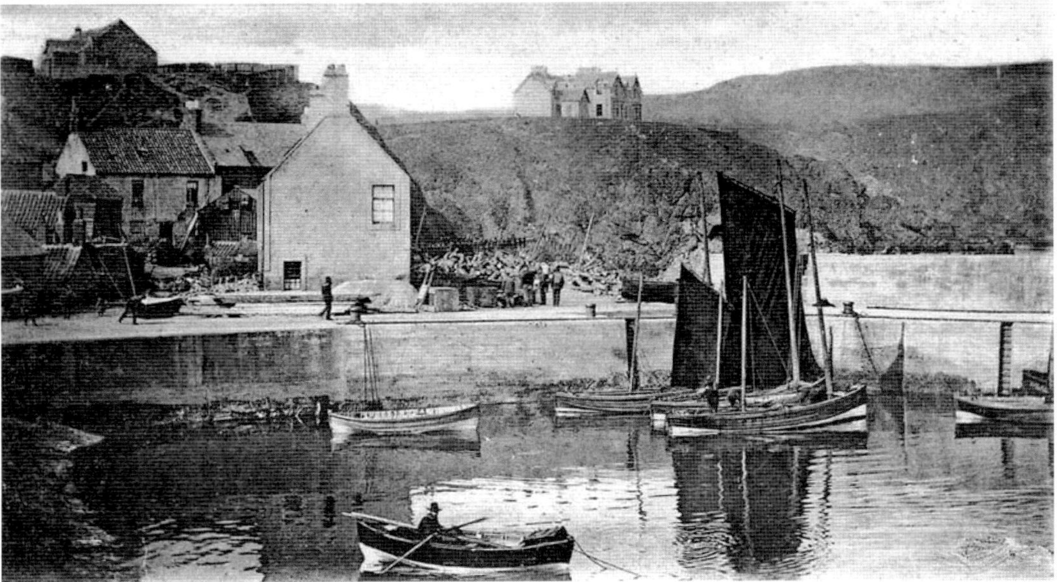

The inner harbour has been built offering protection not only to the fishing craft, but also to the homes of the fishermen. Rock House has been completely rebuilt and even the style of the fishing boats has changed, carrying two sails, although 'punts' were still used for long-lining. Pig bladder floats and nets are hanging up to dry, as well as the villagers' laundry. Piles of lumber sit in front of Rock House, other building materials are on the seaward side and there is a huge pile of blocks in the background behind the nets. Northfield House can be seen in the background, dominating the headland.

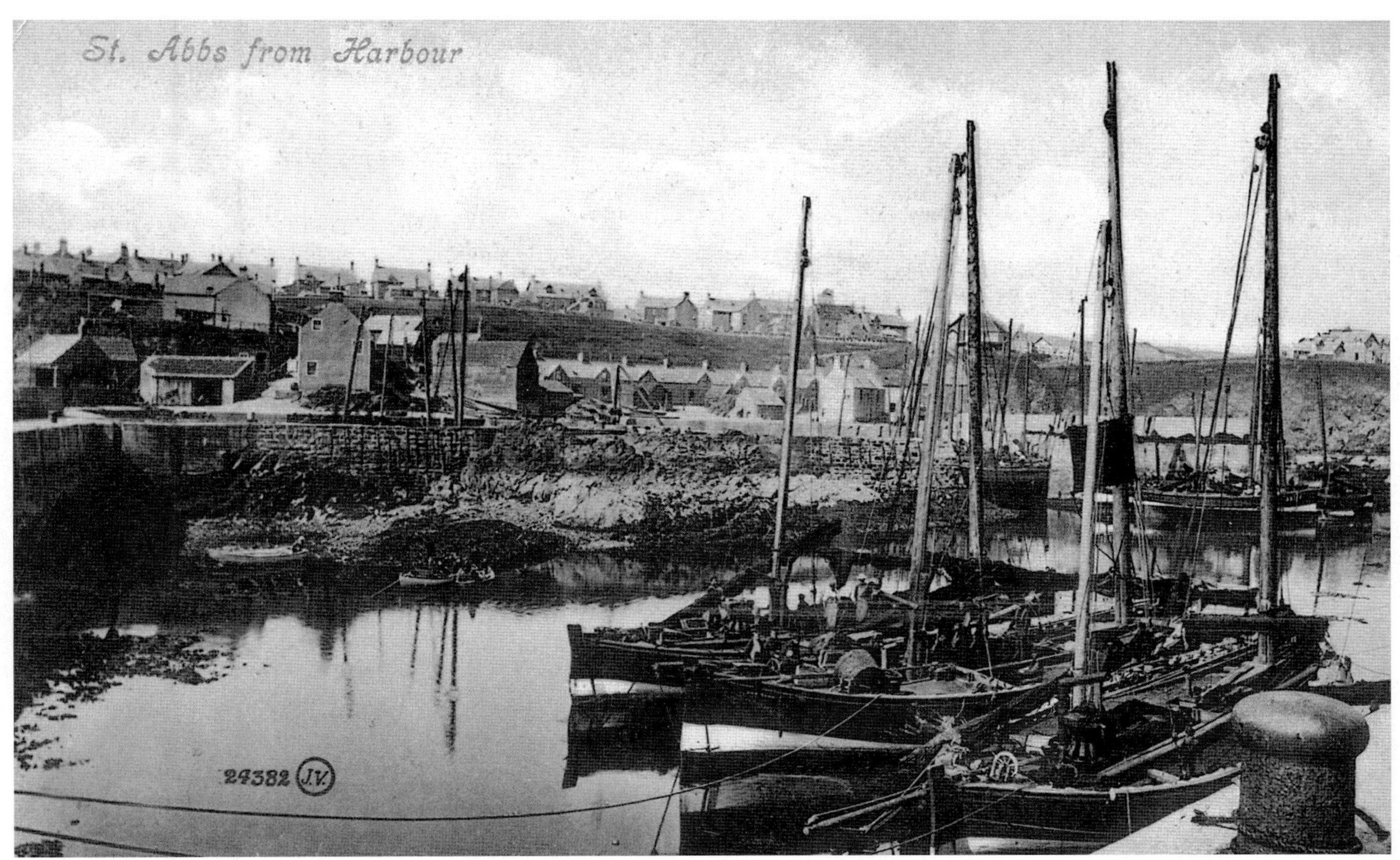

St. Abbs harbour around 1896. The lifeboat slipway or shed have not been built, but bollards are in view in the bottom right corner. The village had prospered well from the herring catches, as the new houses along Briery Law are very prominent. These houses were owned by fishermen. Whilst the main accommodation was rather spacious and modern, many had smaller rooms and a kitchen to the side of the house, beside a small market garden plot, protected from the sea winds by a high wall. During the summer months, the fisherman and his wife and family moved into the smaller buildings and they rented the larger property to the influential friends of Mr. Usher and other wealthy patrons from Edinburgh who loved to 'take the sea air at the Shore'. Judging by the number of the masts in the background, there looks to have been around fifteen boats in the harbour, more likely photographed on a Sunday as these were 'God –feerin' folk' and would not have gone to sea on the Sabbath.

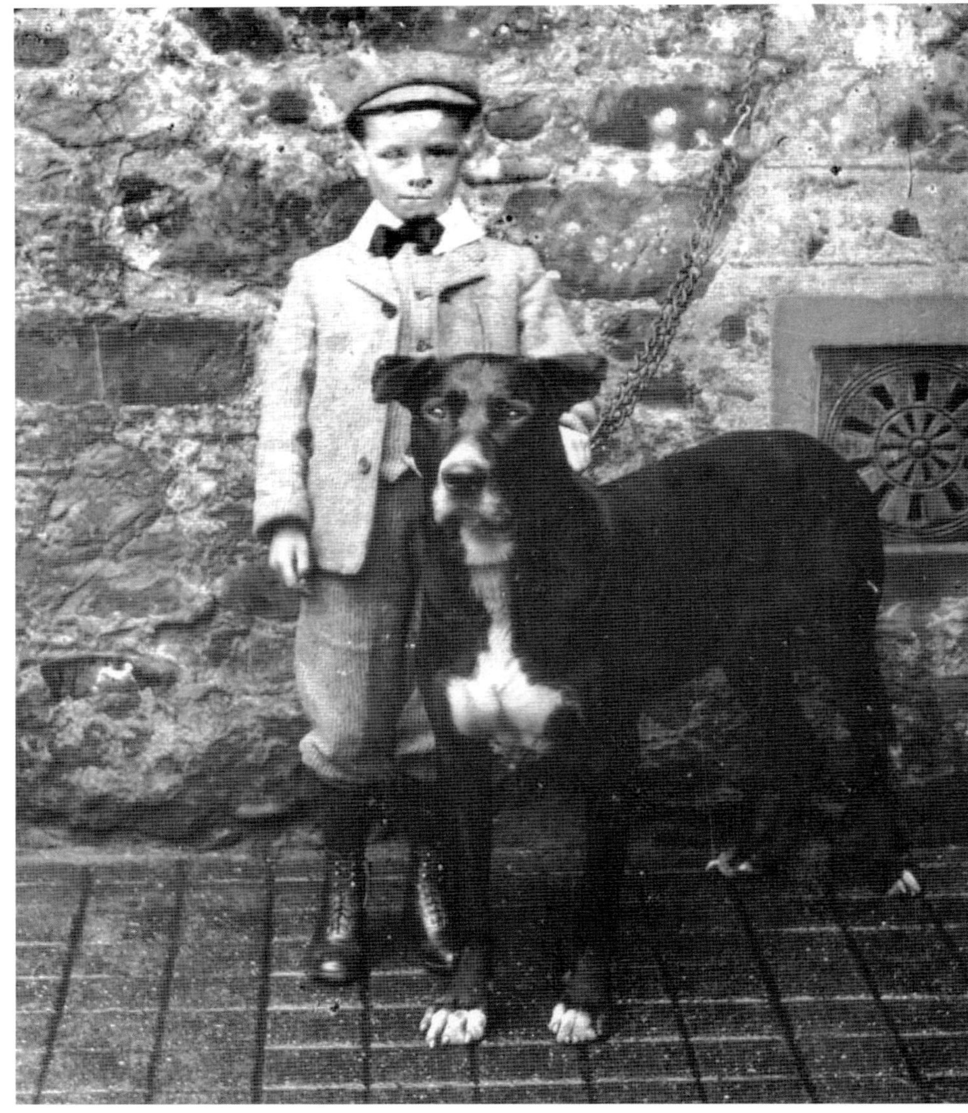

On Thursday 17 October 1907 the Alfred Erlandsen struck the rocks known as Ebb Carrs. Only exposed at low tide, they were a known hazard but were unknown to the captain of the 600 ton Danish steamer. On her way from Riga to Grangemouth carrying a cargo of pit props, deals, and battens for Kirkwood & Co. Glasgow, she was caught in a north-easterly gale combined with thick fog and ran aground. Of the fifteen crew, wife of the captain and their dog, the only survivor was the great dane which managed to swim ashore. It was this calamity which, in conjunction with the improvement to the harbour and the construction of the breakwater brought about the provision of a lifeboat and lifeboat station at St. Abbs. The view shows the great dane, renamed Carro (after the Carr Rocks) and a boy whose name is unknown.

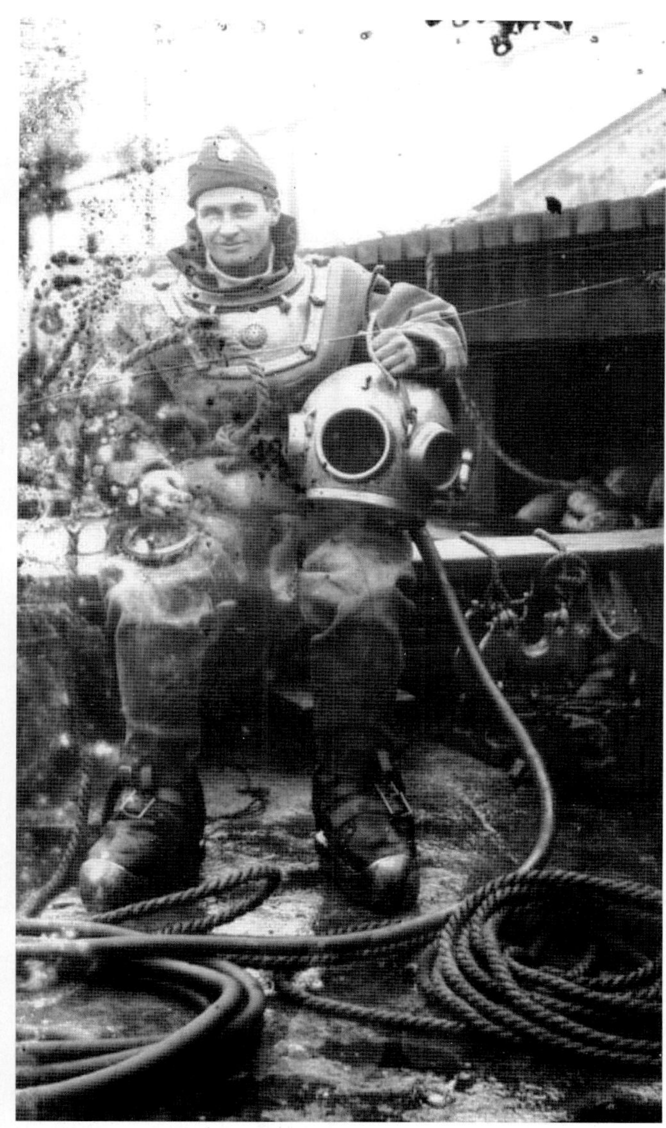

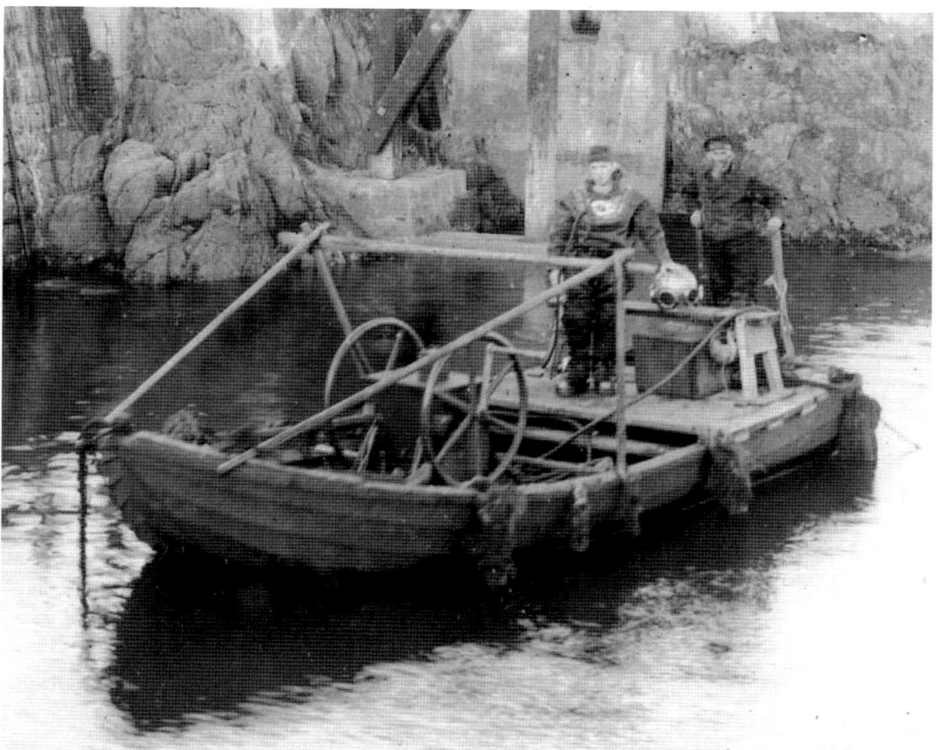

This was a professional diver of the time, employed with three others to salvage as much of the Alfred Erlandsen as possible. Fitted with the very latest canvas suits, big lead boots and a brass helmet, the air supply was supplied by umbilical cord to the surface where a pair of stout lads would hand crank the Siebe Gorman hand pump. Two of the St. Abbs locals were also employed as salvage divers. Peter Ray and George 'Coco' Wilson undertook much of the work around the treacherous Ebb Carrs. What remains of the shipwreck is covered in soft corals, anemones and kelp and is very popular with visiting scuba divers.

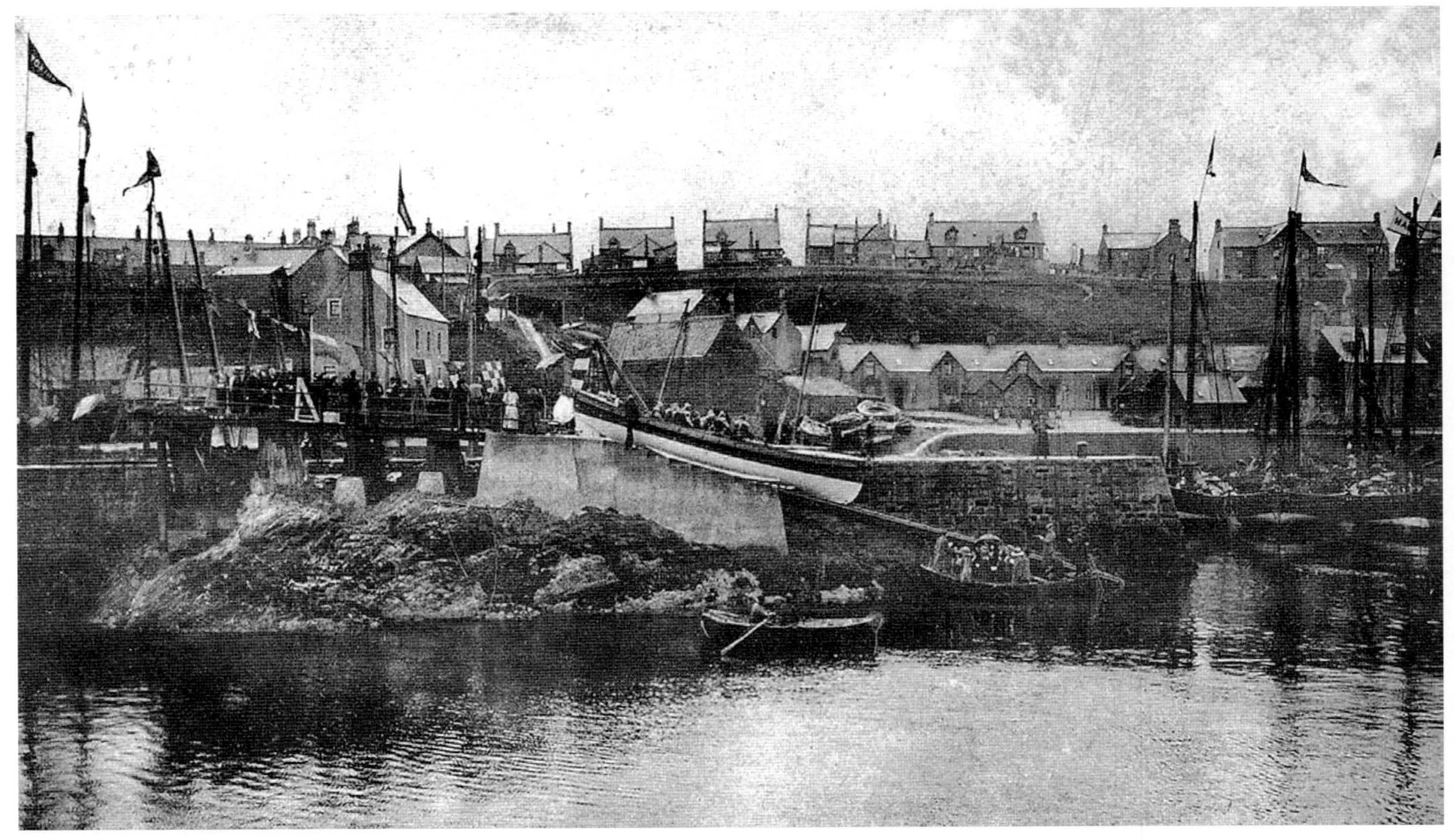

Following the sinking of the Alfred Erlandsen on Thursday 17 October 1907 and the tragic loss of life on the Ebb Carr Rocks, the RNLI proposed that a lifeboat station should be erected within St. Abbs new harbour. Construction followed quickly, making use of one of the inner harbour walls and a natural hard rock foundation. The *Helen Smitton* was launched on 25 April 1911 amidst great fanfare on what was a 'gae dreech day'. Protecting their cameras with umbrellas as well as the tender sensibilities of the ladies present, the *Helen Smitton* rolled down the slipway into St. Abbs harbour.

Below: James Wilson.

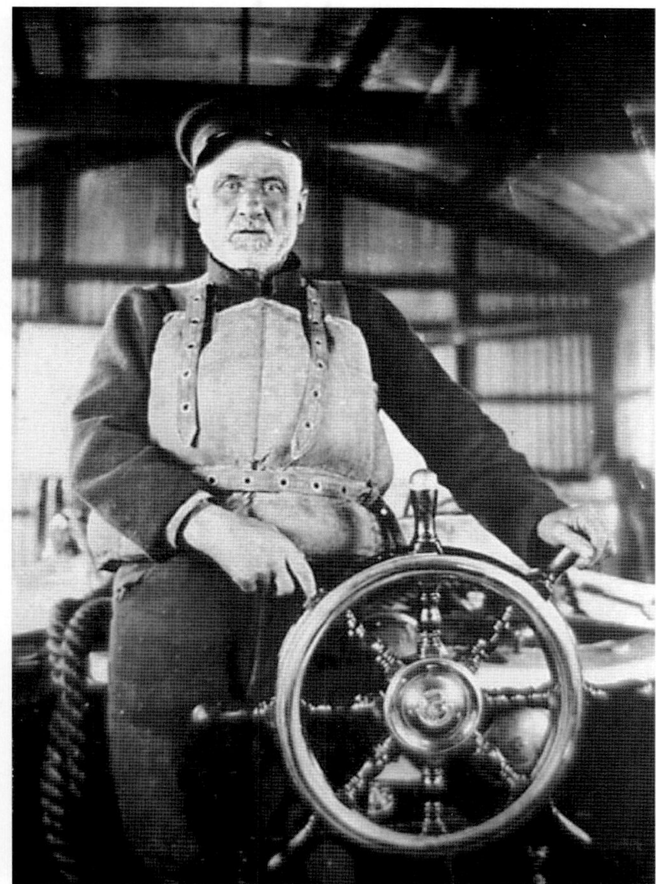

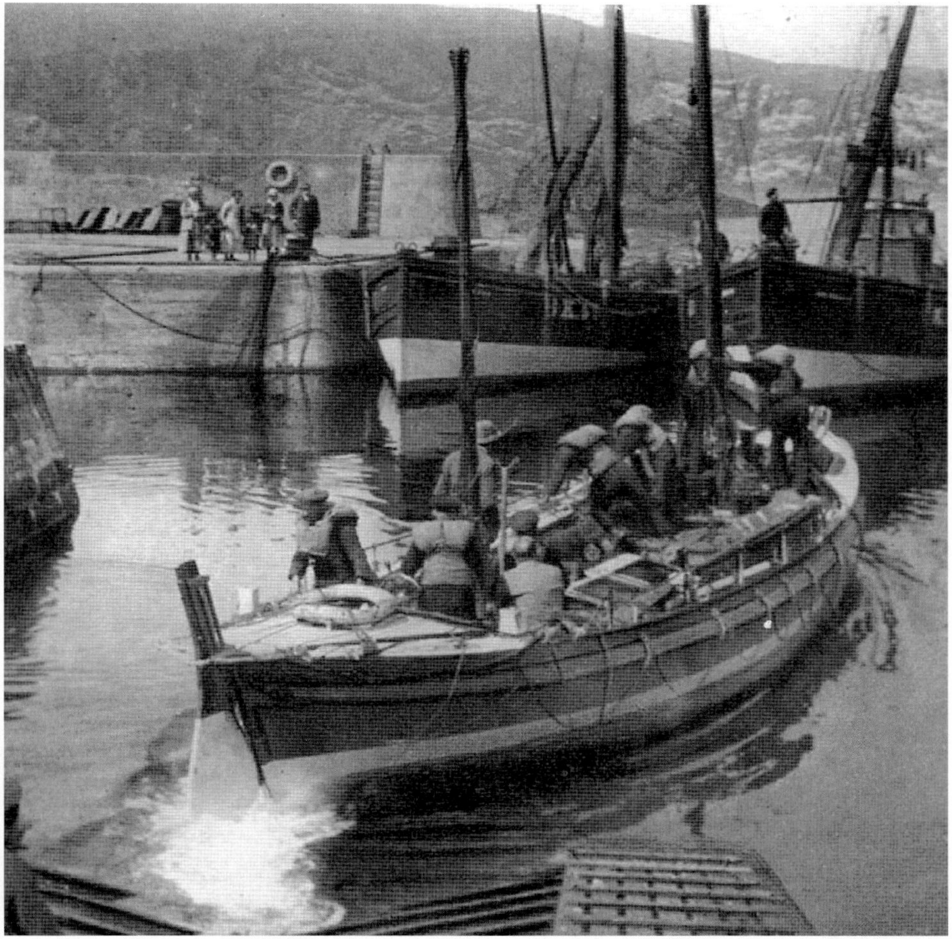

The *Helen Smitton's* official number was 603 and she was built by Thomas Ironworks, Rowedge, in 1910 at a cost of £3,563. The money was provided as a donor legacy by James Hodge of Manchester. The *Helen Smitton* was a non-self righting type Watson Motor Boat, fitted with a 24hp Wolsley 4 cylinder engine, capable of 7.5 knots. She was 38ft in length, had a 10ft beam and was fitted with a 21 inch Villinger reversible propeller. During her illustrious career she had 27 service launches and was responsible for saving 37 lives. She had two coxswains, James Wilson who served from 1911 to 1931 and James Nisbet who served from 1931 to 1936.

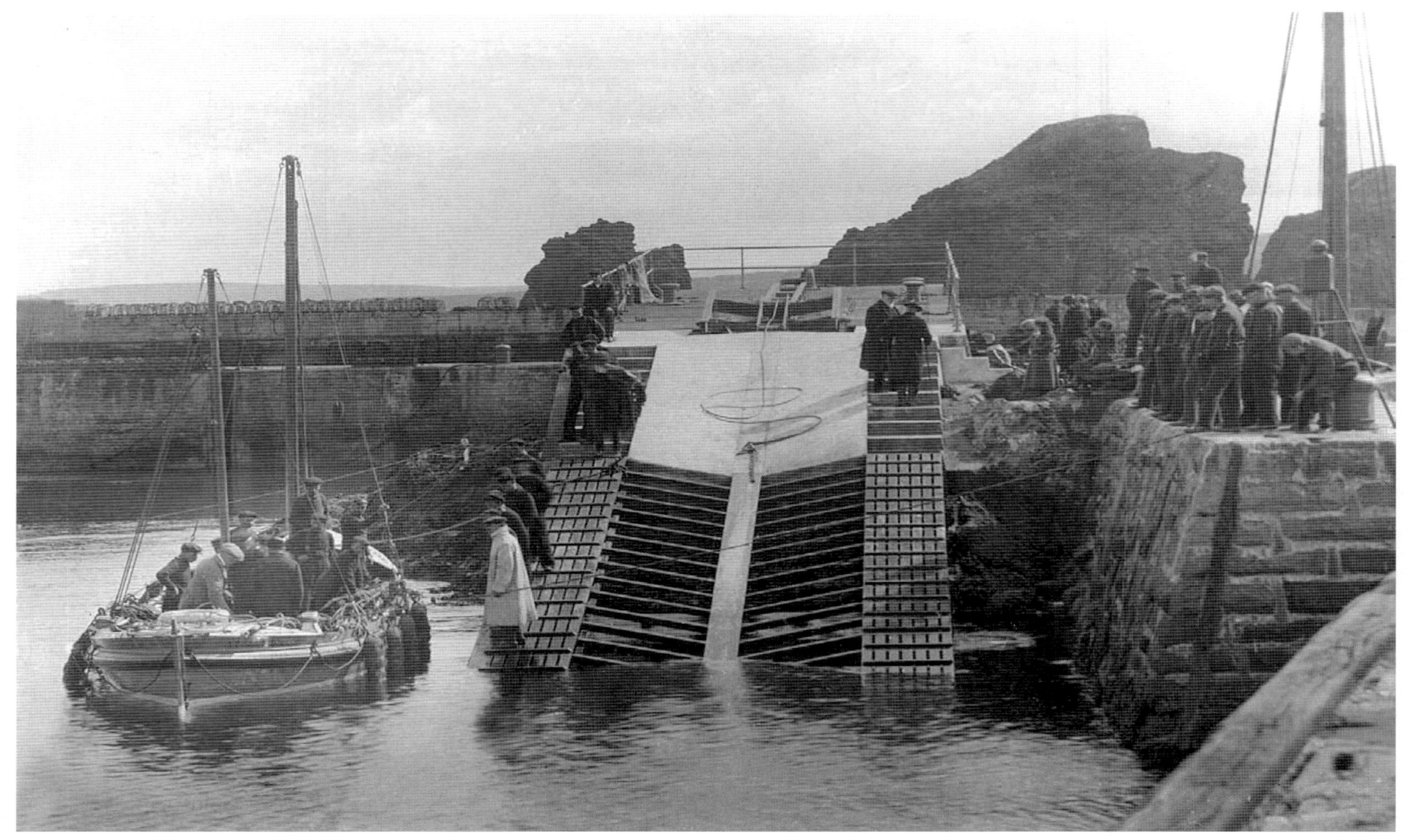

The first crew were James Wilson:- 1st Cox; James Nisbet:- 2nd Cox; William Laing:- Bowman; Tom Cormack:- Mechanic and John Nisbet:- Crew. It took a few more years before the lifeboat shed was built to house the lifeboat and it is still fundamentally the same today. The slipway faces out to the harbour mouth. The current lifeboat is of the inshore type inflatable Atlantic 75, fitted with twin 70hp Yamaha outboard engines and is called the *Dorothy and Catherine Barr II*, donated by the Barr Trust.

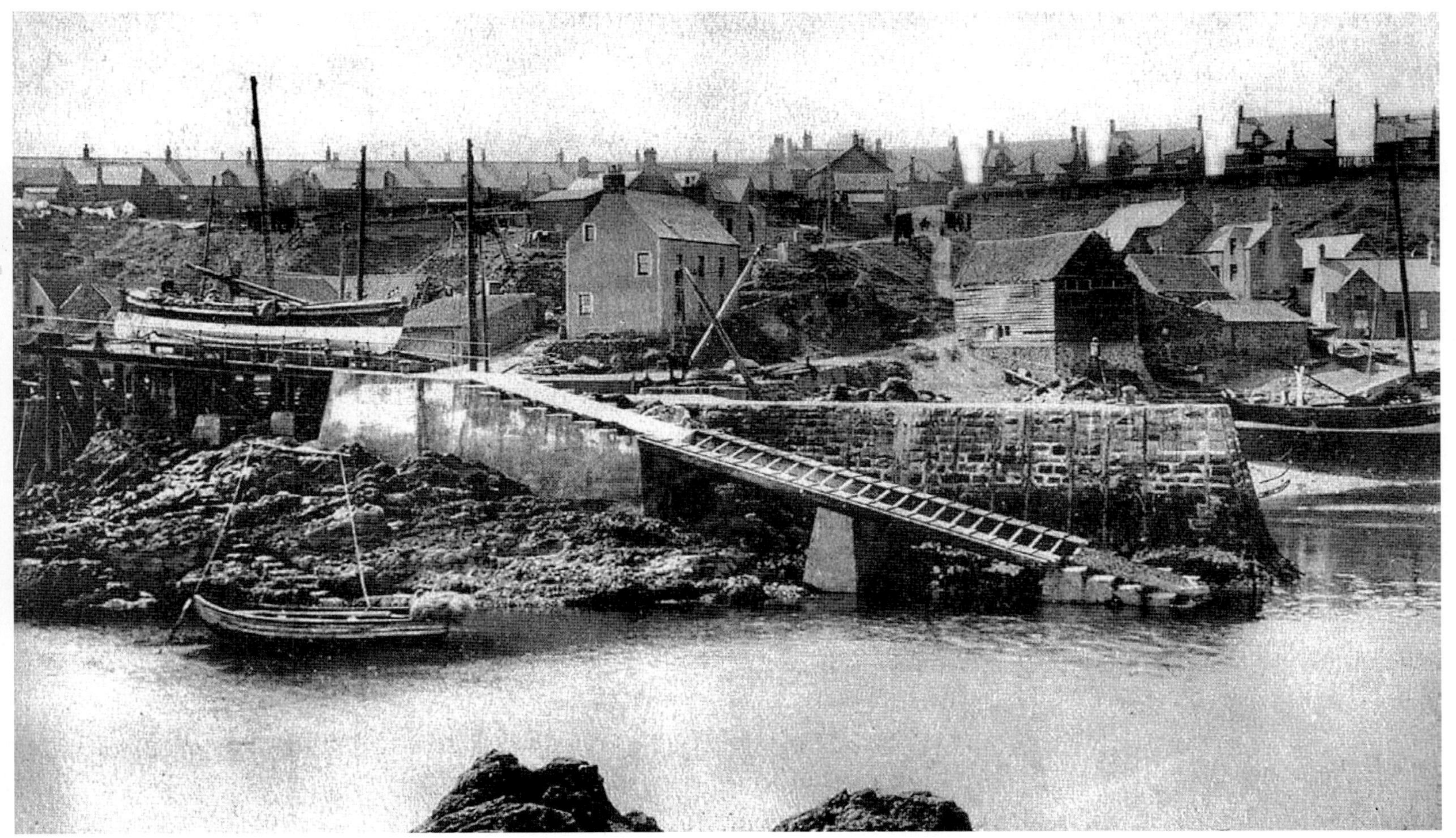

Here the lifeboat *Helen Smitton* is at rest, up on her blocks but still exposed to the ravages of the weather. The large building behind, at the foot of the road leading down to the harbour, is showing obvious signs of deterioration, with planks of wood missing, holes in the walls and window glass gone in the upper part. It would not be long before this old net store would come down and stay down, never being replaced. The lifeboat was almost impossible to launch at low tide, so her slipway ramp was extended further when the shed was built. Now, with the shallow draft of the current lifeboat, it can be launched in any state of tide.

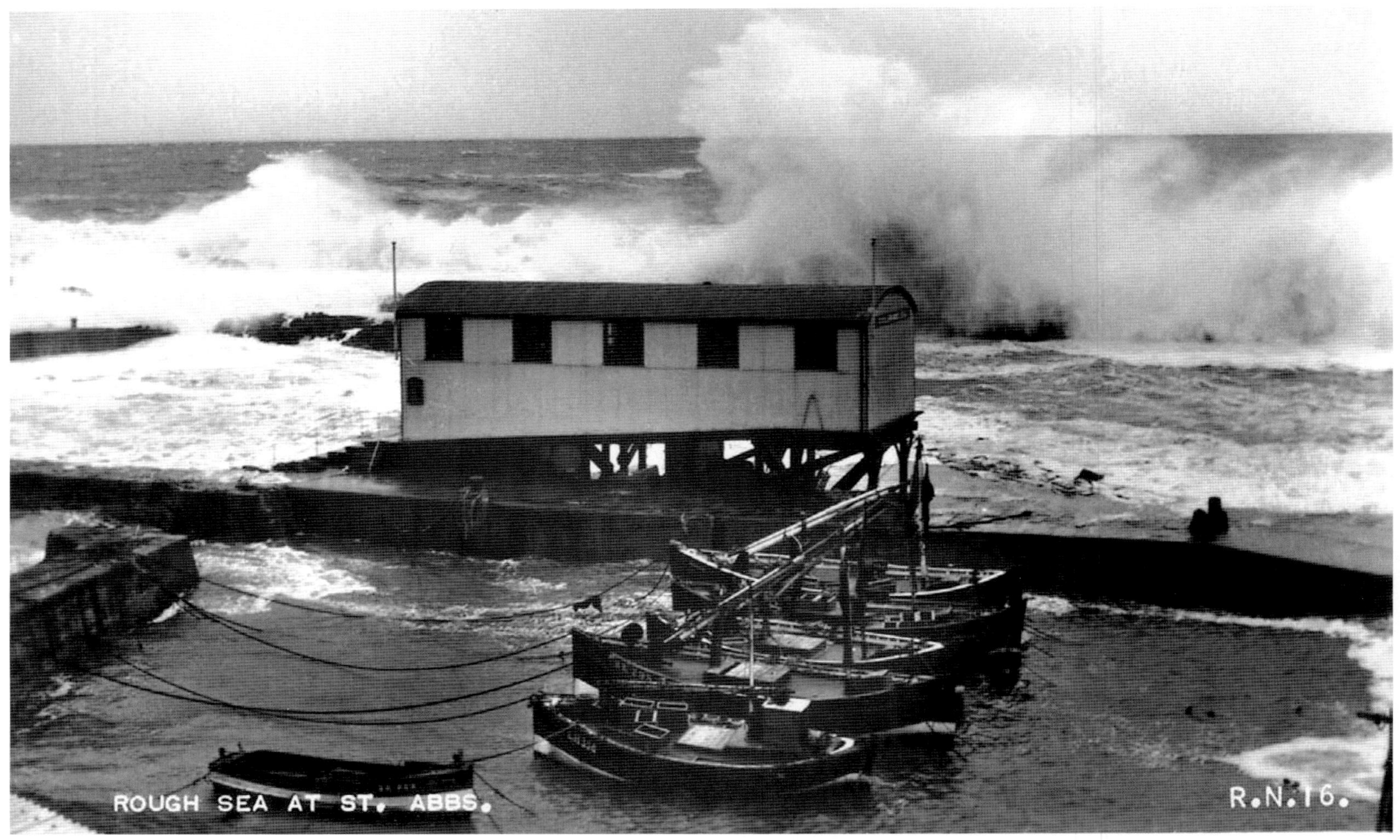

Here we see the might of the North Sea in all her fury. The newly constructed lifeboat shed is dwarfed by the height of the wave as it crashes over the protective sea wall. Part of the fishing fleet have been pulled into the inner harbour, which at one time had protective gates which acted as a coffer dam. The original inner harbour was first built in 1833, at a cost of £1,200 and was able to protect sixteen boats. It is still the safest place for any craft during the worst of the winter storms.

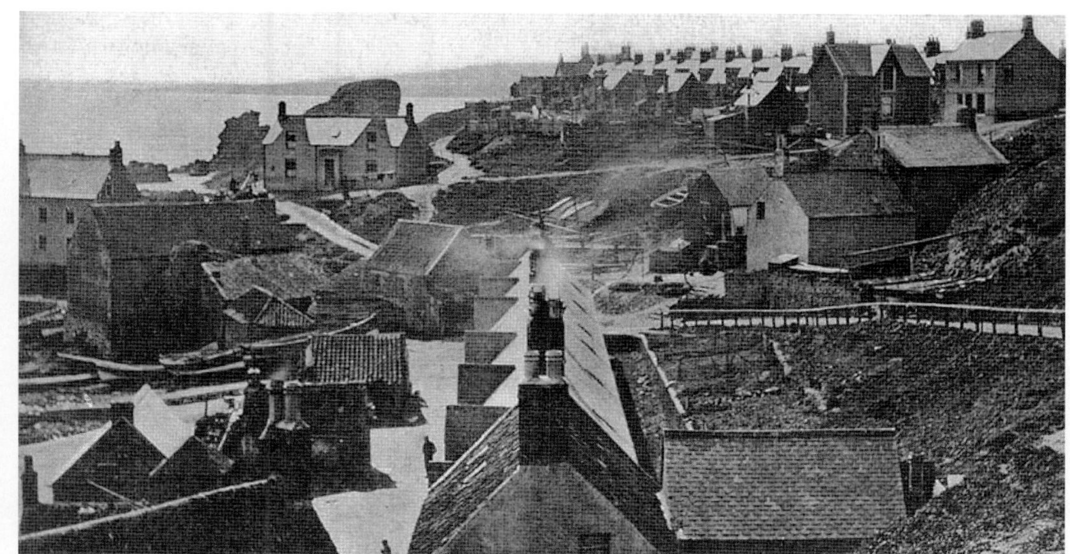

A rather smoky scene of lower St. Abbs, still showing the Under Row, now a car park. The fireplaces were originally placed in the centre of the room, but as renovations were made over the years, the old clat and clay homes had to be pulled down due to the ravages of the sea and replaced with brick and blockwork. The fireplaces were then moved to the gable ends of the houses. Whilst this looks like a fairly modern photograph, one vital clue to the age is in the middle left. There is a large building once used as a net store, which juts into the harbour area. Sirus House is behind, but the building in front, which incorporated the local bedrock as part of her walls, has been absent almost 100 years.

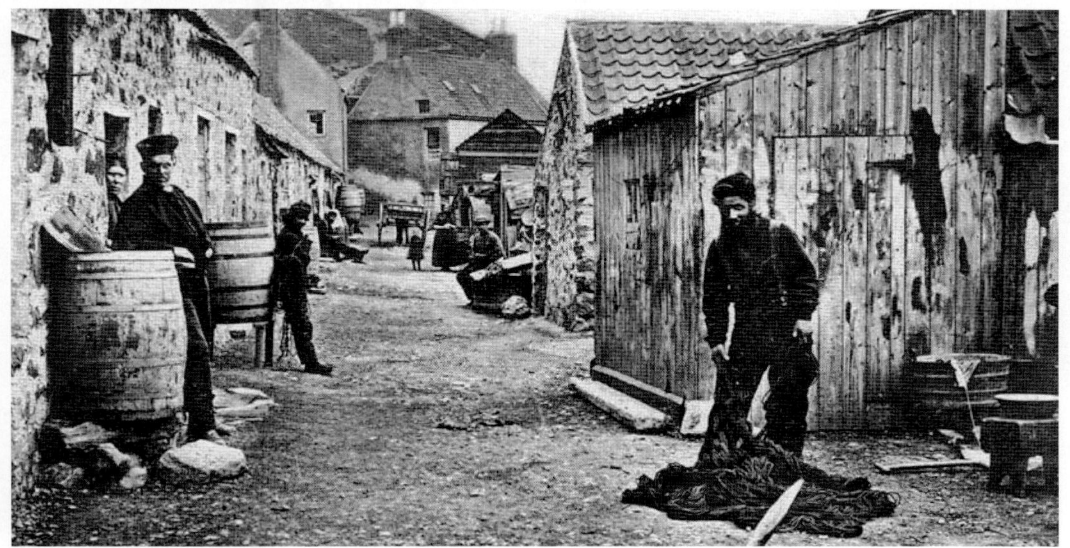

This was a typical 'staged' scene for the visiting photographer, who probably has just interrupted the day's business, as there is one of the fishmen standing over his hemp ropes. The houses have water barrels as there was no running water. All East Coast fishermen wore the distinctive headgear seen here.

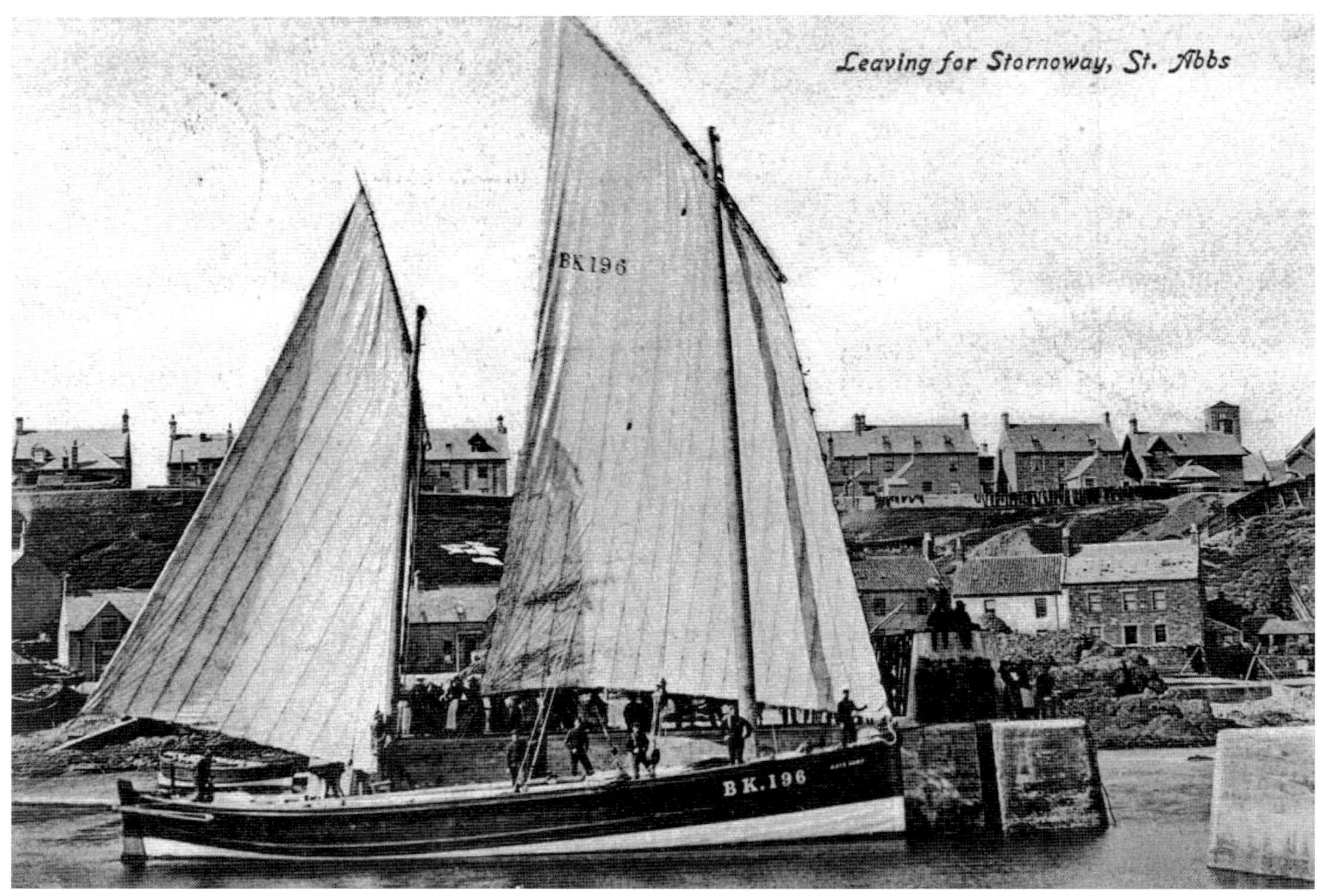

At the height of the fishing season, the advancing shoals of herring that moved up the east coast of Britain, brought fishing craft from all over to catch the "silver darlings". Local boats would frequently leave very early in the season to travel to the west coast of Scotland and would be gone for months at a time. Here the view is of one of the 'Fifie's' leaving St. Abbs for Stornoway in the Outer Hebrides. Many of the local women also followed the herring fleet as it advanced around our shores, travelling by train wherever possible, or by horse & cart, as they had their belongings with them, packed tightly in a 'kist'.

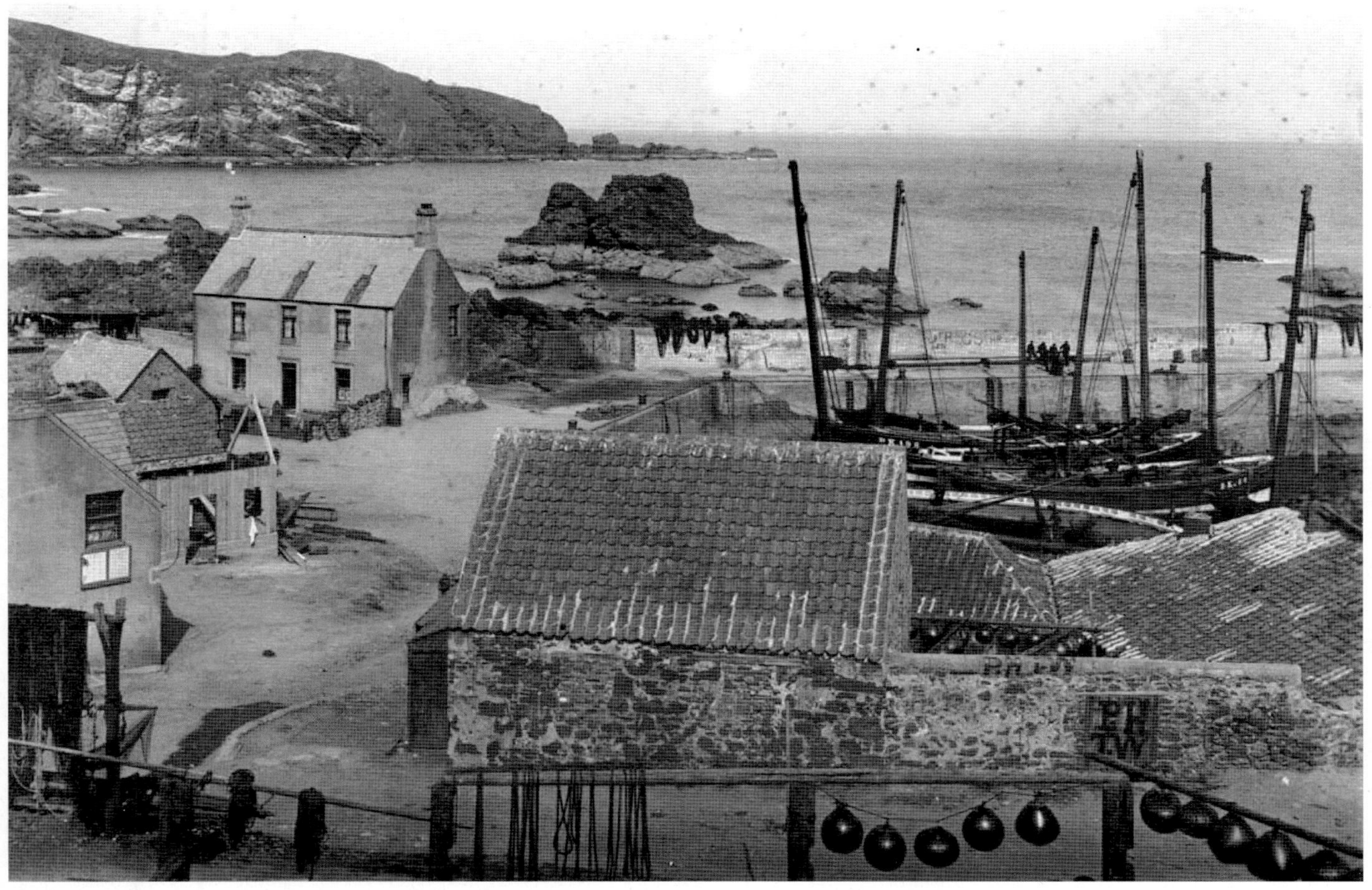

This view has changed little, except for the removal of the Under Row. The gable end of the last property can just be seen to the left of the photograph. The net store in front is now a licensed café and the attendant buildings are also still standing. The small wooden sheds near the houses remain also, but this photograph shows so much more of the lives of the locals. Animal bladder floats and nets are hanging up to dry and a group of fishermen are sitting on a ship's mast against the far harbour wall, as they tend to their nets and fishing lines. A few boats are at rest, but what is interesting is what we would call graffiti. With so many 'foreign' boats using the harbour, the local fishermen daubed the harbour wall with their initials in black paint to show which was the boat's berth and to indicate which net store belonged to which boat.

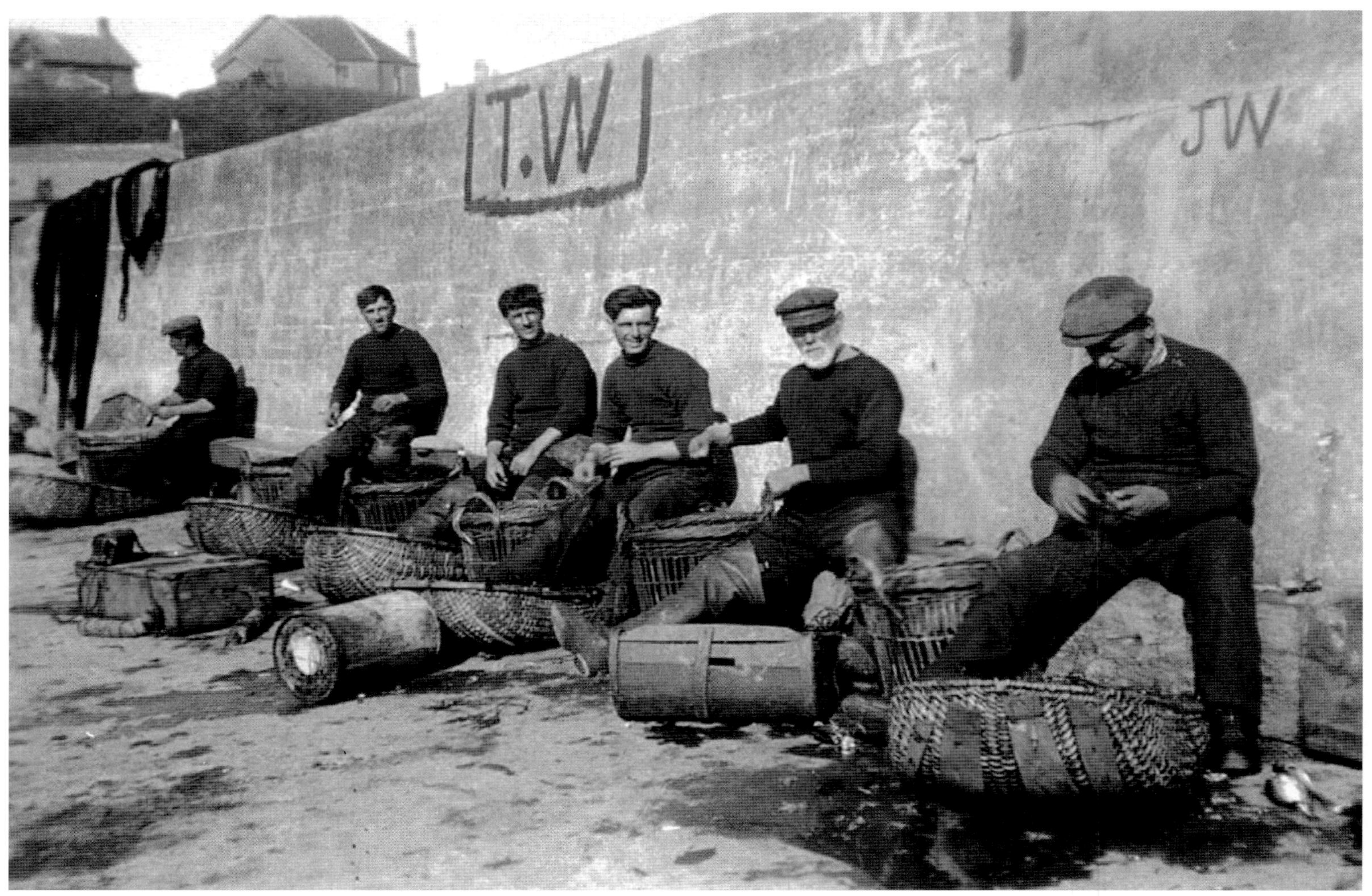

Here a group of St. Abbs callants are baiting the lines in their skulls. Using mussels collected along the foreshore, the hundreds of long lines were inspected and repaired each time they were used. Hooks were replaced and the mussel meat was secured in readiness for going to fish for cod, pollack, ling, and the mackerel which swarm into the bay in their thousands during the summer months.

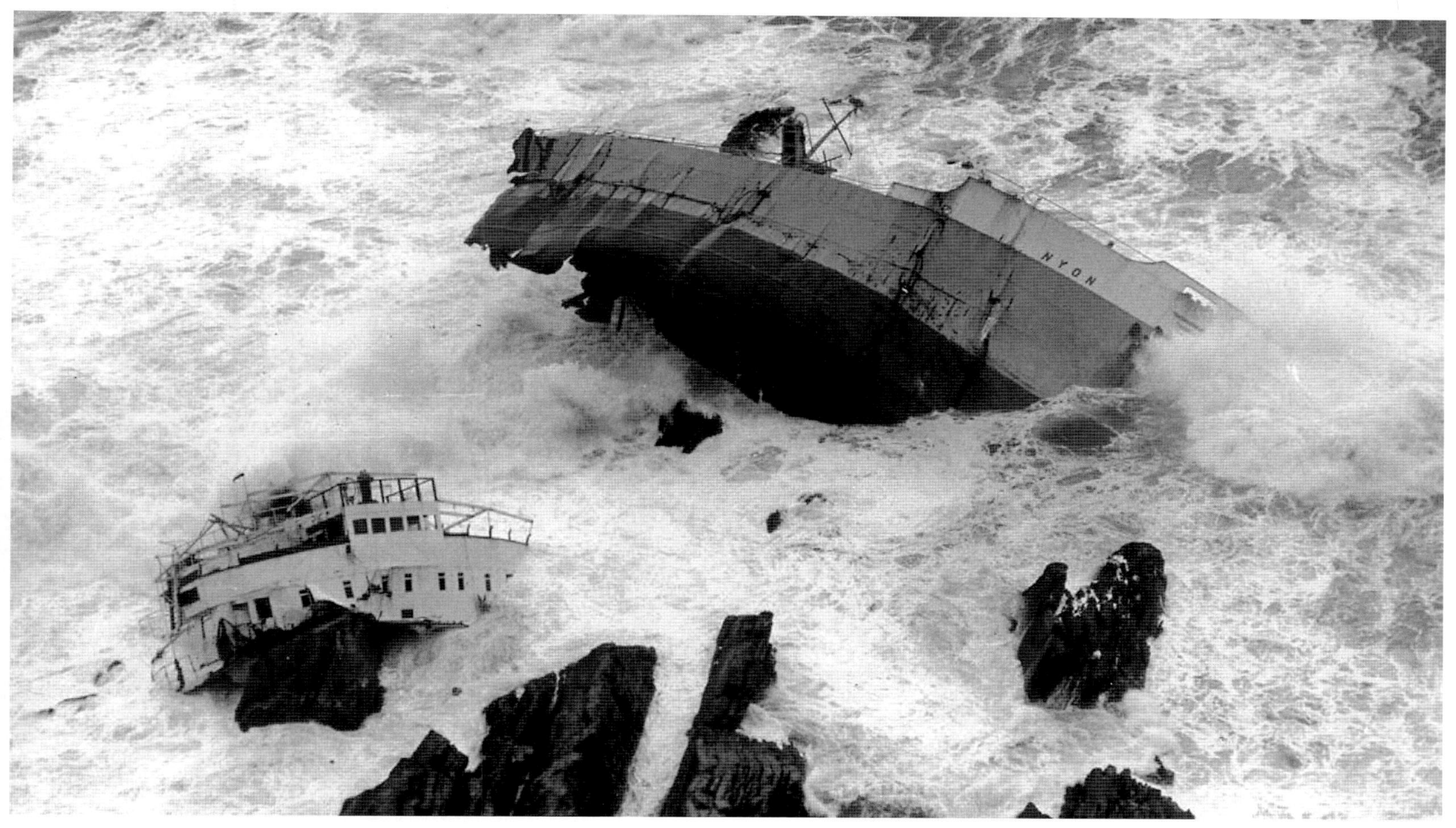

On 17 November 1958 the 4,950-ton Swiss motor vessel *Nyon*, on its way from Leith to Dakar struck Meg Watson's Rock near Fast Castle, 4 miles north of St. Abbs Head. The Following day, the St. Abbs Branch of the Board of Trade Life Saving Association made a daring rescue by firing a line by rocket from the cliff tops over to the *Nyon*. The crew managed to attach a steel hawser to rig up a breeches buoy to rescue all of the crew. The St. Abbs Lifeboat manned by coxwain James Wilson, established an RNLI record by standing by at the scene of the wreck from 18 to 27 November. The rear section of the ship was cut off and was to be towed to Rotterdam but sank in a collision near Beachy Head. The foresection was soon dashed to pieces under the relentless North Sea swell.

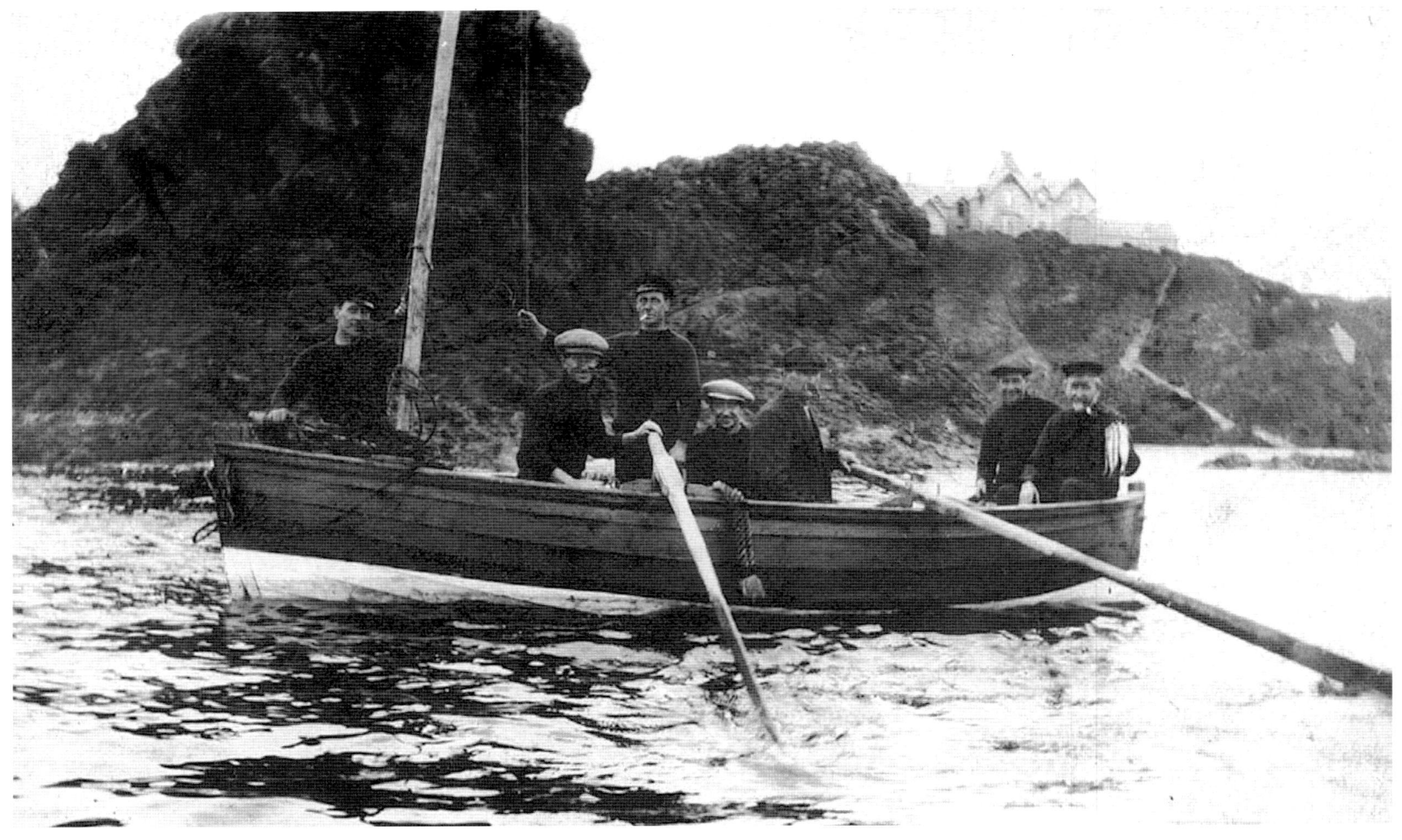

This is typical of the small inshore boat used for long-line fishing. Fitted with a detachable single mast and four oars, it could easily accommodate six men, all armed with hundreds of lines to catch fish. The boats were used to set the lobster pots and salmon nets as well as for ferrying the catch ashore from the larger fishing boats when the tide was too low for entry into the harbour. The men are rowing past Maw Carr just outside the entrance to the harbour. This rock is also known as Seagull Rock.

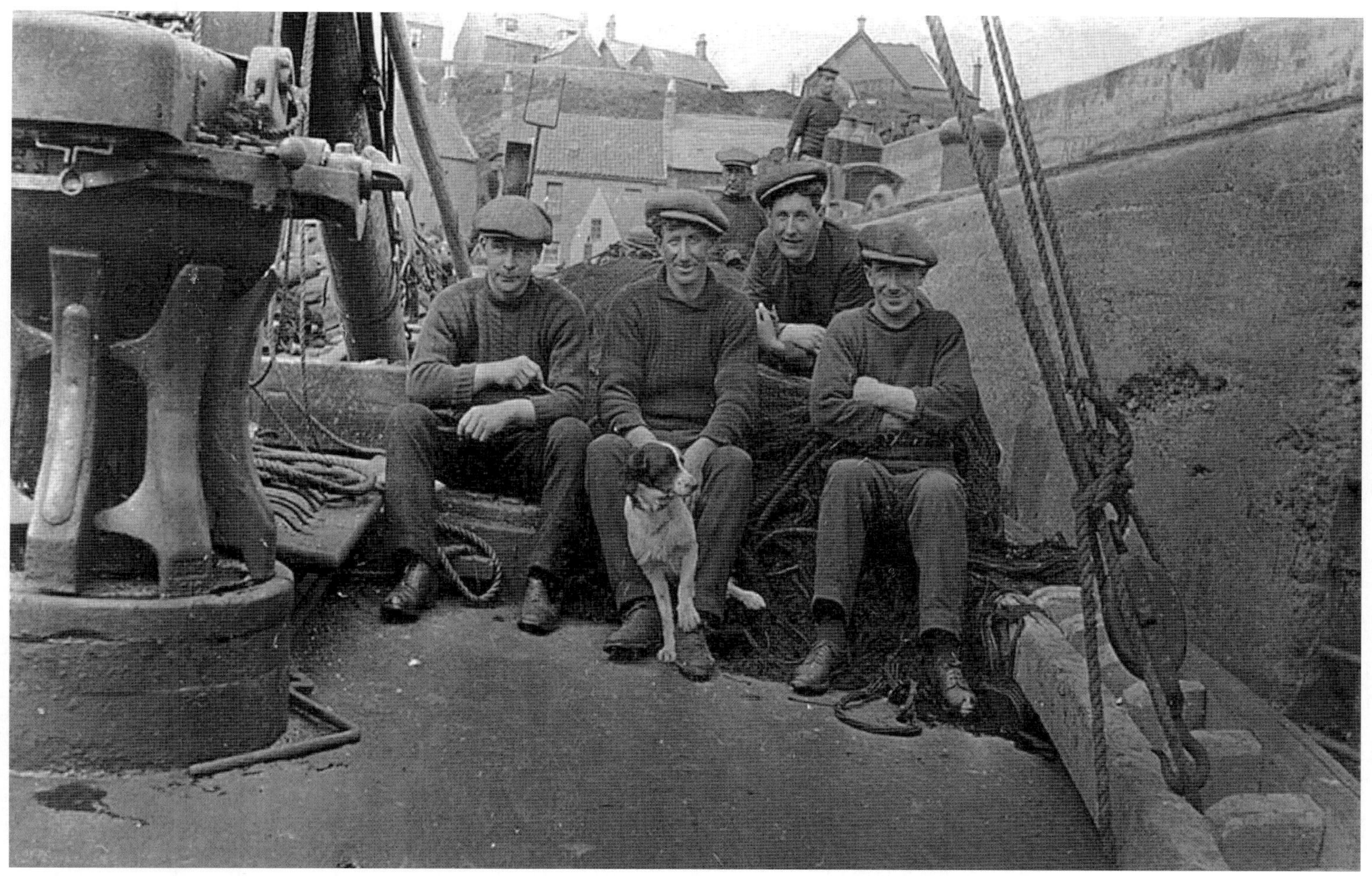

These young fishermen are on one of the newer fishing boats, as witnessed by the steam-driven capstan on the foredeck of the drifter. From left to right are Peter Hood; Peter Hood; ?... Hood; Peter Wilson and a dog named Earl. Steam drifters were a natural progression from sail and indeed there were several different types of sailing vessel too, all of them designed to be more and more efficient at catching and storing fish. The boat builders J. Weatherhead of Eyemouth were the first company to build boats with closed in decks, allowing for storage of fish below. It was these radical new designs which were built with one thing in mind!

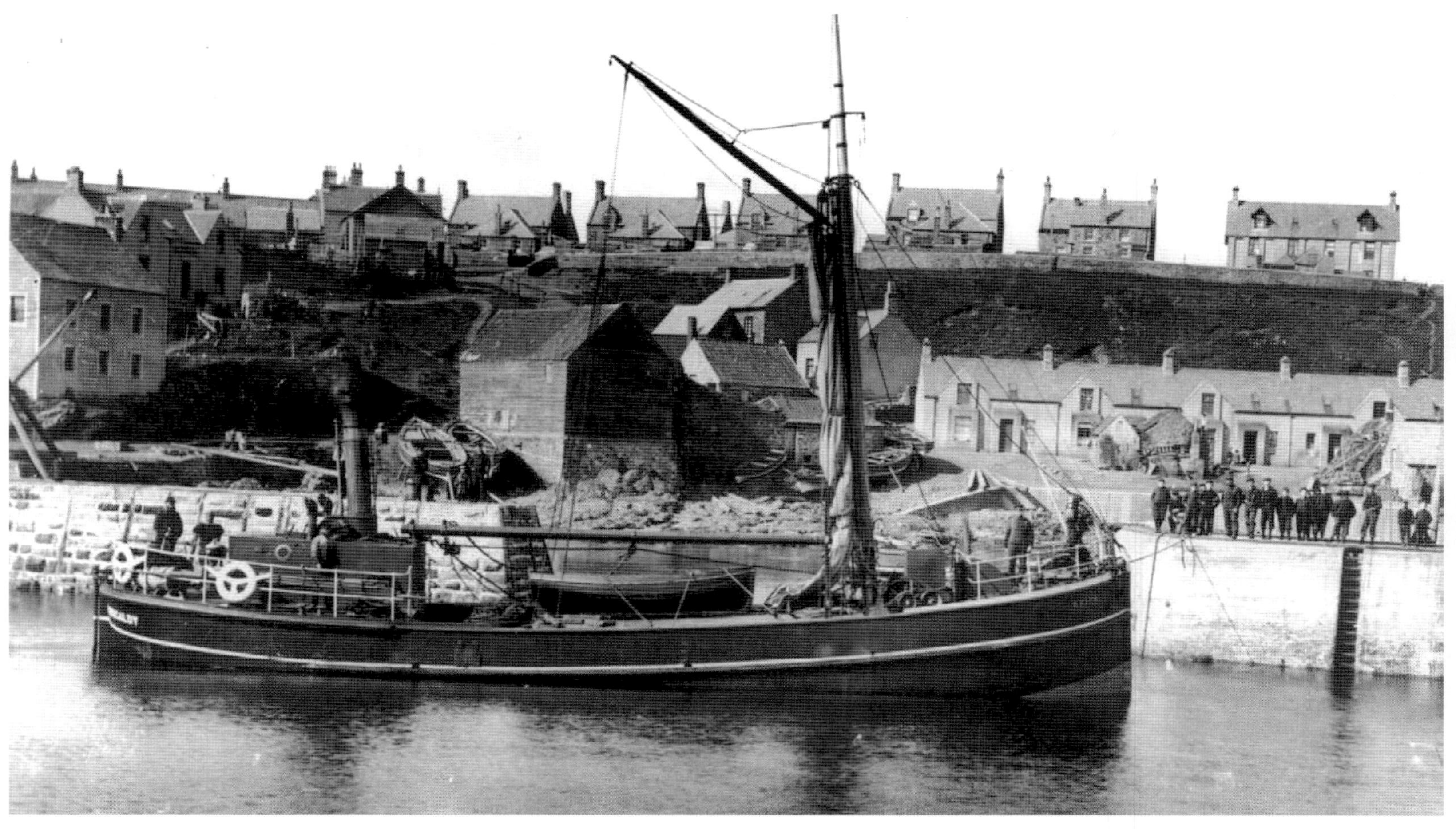

Photographed by John Wood in 1900, the small steam coaster *S.S. Raith* was a regular visitor to St. Abbs. Built by John Scott & Co. at Kinghorn, Fife in 1895 for the local ship owners Theb Kirkcaldy, Leith & Glasgow Steam Packet Co. Ltd. of Kirkcaldy, she could carry a dead weight of 150 tons of a variety of products such as grain, coal, stone or even flax for the linoleum industry in Kirkcaldy. She was a single screw vessel built of steel, was 66ft. long, 18ft. 2ins. in beam and had a loaded draft of 8ft. 8ins. The *S.S. Raith* had a single cylinder steam engine of 20 hp. built by the shipbuilders at their Kirkcaldy engine works which gave a speed of around 7 knots. She worked steadily until 1919 when she was struck by heavy seas carrying a cargo of coal off Aberdeen. The crew was saved, but the ship was lost.

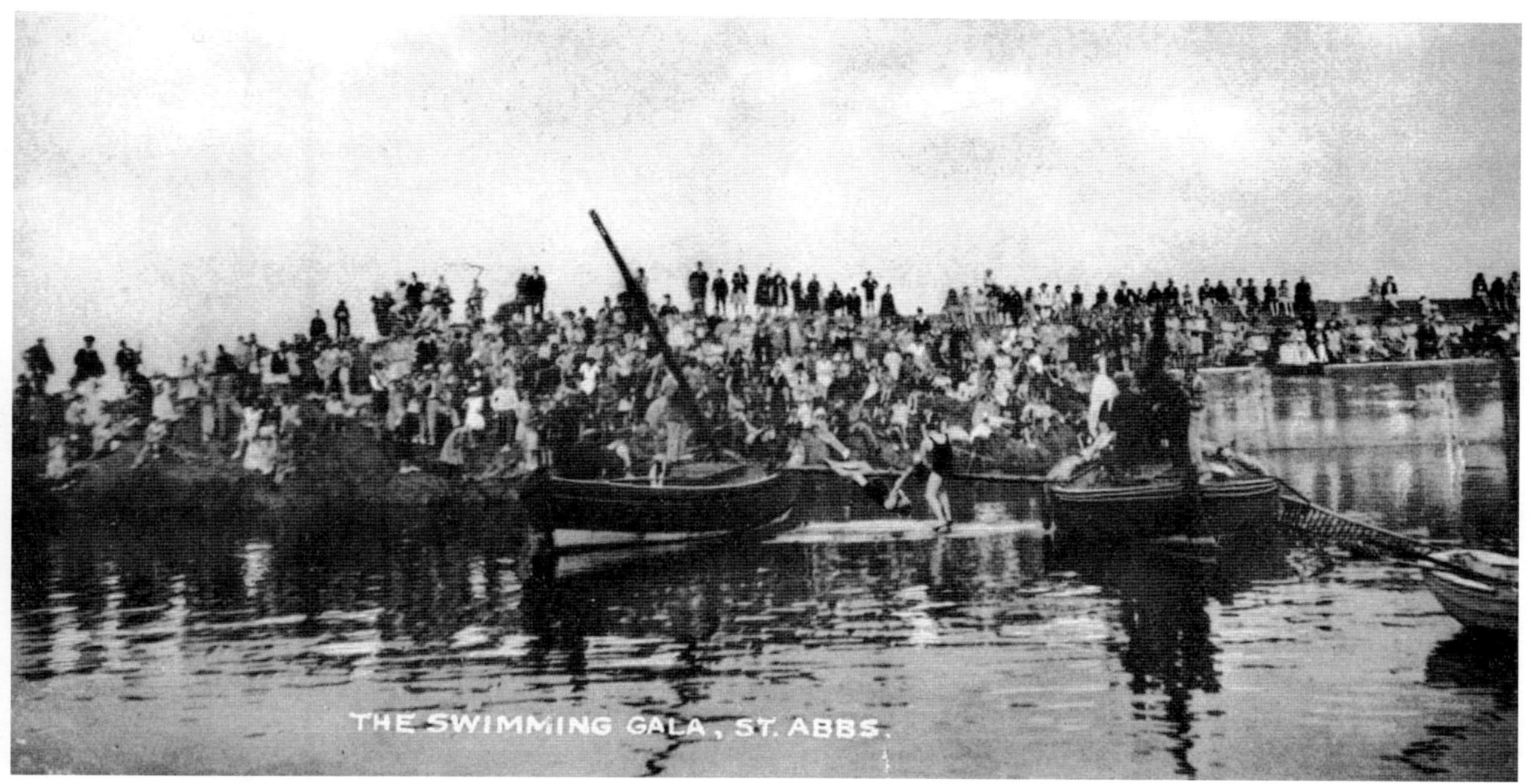

Whilst this may not be the clearest of pictures, it recalls a way of life and community in the local villages. Taking place in the outer harbour is part of a grand swimming gala. The rocks and harbour side are filled with locals and tourists alike and two combatants are getting to grips on a slippery mast stretched between two of the smaller punts. Obviously at the height of the summer, and always on a Sunday, the water must have been warm enough to swim in and from the looks of the photograph, one of the team members is losing his balance and is in the process of falling in the water. Now a local festival revolves around the lifeboat and all the village families get together, but no-one goes into the water as part of a Gala now, only scuba divers who visit the St. Abbs & Eyemouth Voluntary Marine Nature Reserve. It is thought that this swimming gala harkened back to the old days when there was a fair held in St. Abbs in July of each year. The fishermen and their wives erected stalls along the front of the Under Row where gingerbread and other sweetmeats were sold to visitors and handed out to children. Various items of clothing that had been knitted, crocheted or woven over the winter months were also sold.

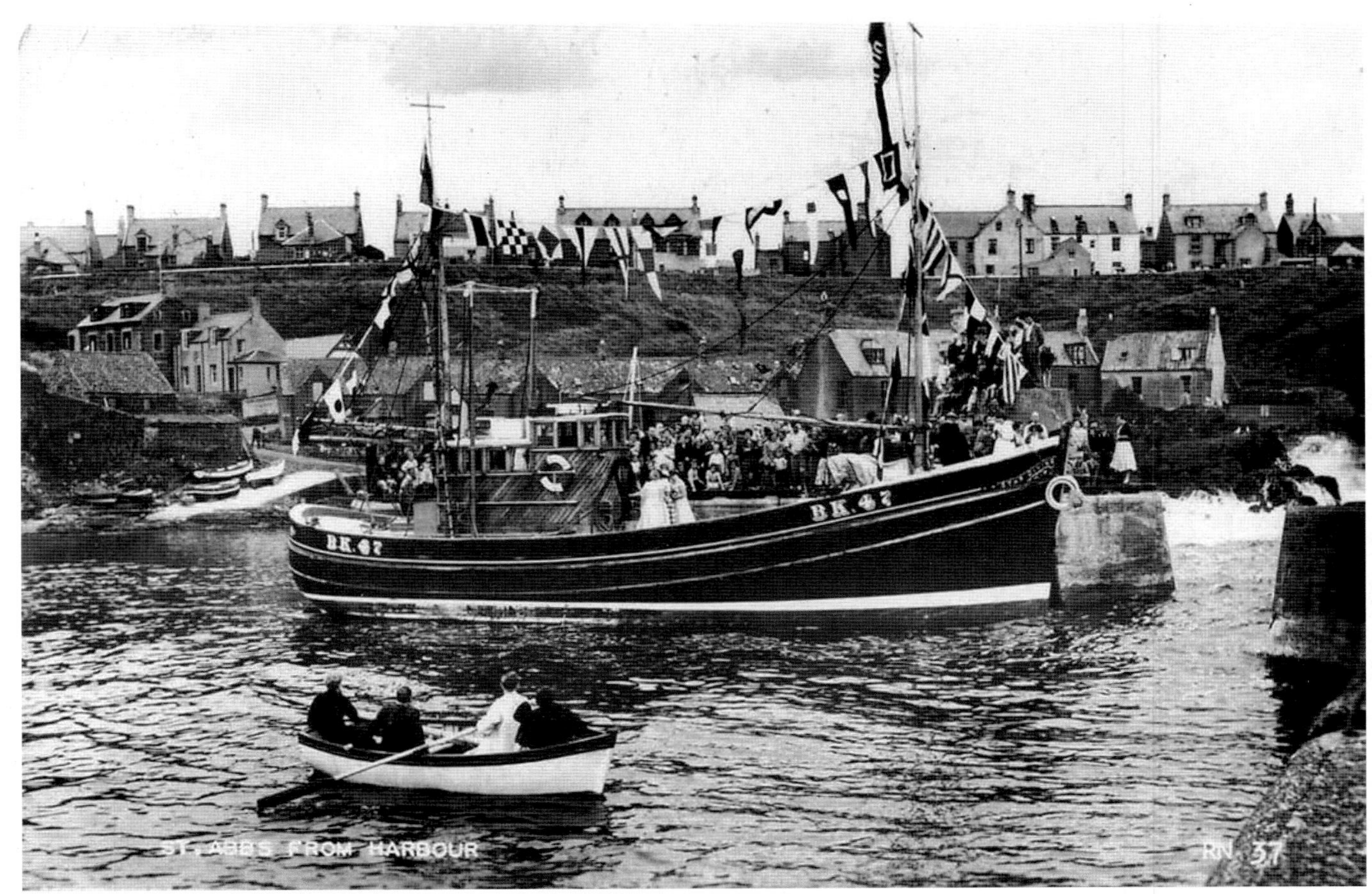

Seen here is the start of the Herring Queen Festival, which is in fact an Eyemouth festival, held in July each year, and comes as a celebration of the old herring industry. The Herring Queen is chosen from amongst her schoolfriends in Eyemouth High School, which is the senior school also for St. Abbs & Coldingham. The festival starts off at St. Abbs Harbour, where the person chosen to be crowned and her Maids of Honour travel to St. Abbs Harbour. There they are picked up by one of the local fishing boats, bedecked in bunting, and carried to Eyemouth some two miles by sea, accompanied by most of the fishing fleet as well as the inshore lifeboat from St. Abbs and the offshore lifeboat from Eyemouth. There the Herring Queen is crowned by a local dignitary or special guest and a week of festivities follows.This photograph, produced as a postcard by Robbie Nisbet depicts the local Herring Queen Festival and the close ties between Eyemouth and St. Abbs.